JUMBLE

Jackpot

The Winning Combination
for Puzzle Fun

Henri Arnold, Bob Lee,
and Mike Argirion

TRIUMPH
BOOKS
CHICAGO

This book is available in quantity at special discounts
for your group or organization.

For further information, contact:

Triumph Books
542 South Dearborn Street
Suite 750
Chicago, Illinois 60605
(312) 939-3330
Fax (312) 663-3557

Printed in U.S.A.

ISBN-13: 978-1-57243-897-2
ISBN-10: 1-57243-897-5

Design by Sue Knopf

CONTENTS

Classic Puzzles

Daily Puzzles

Challenger Puzzles

Answers

JUMBLE®

Unscramble these four Jumbles, one letter to each square, to form four ordinary words.

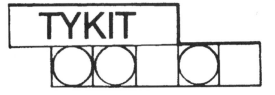

TYKIT

ENNIL

PERMAC

ONSOAL

I come to bury Caesar. . .

WHAT THE ANCIENT ROMANS COULD DO EASILY THAT MOST MODERNS HAVE DIFFICULTY DOING.

Now arrange the circled letters to form the surprise answer, as suggested by the above cartoon.

Print answer here

JUMBLE®

Unscramble these four Jumbles, one letter to
each square, to form four ordinary words.

OPTIA

ROUCS

CARCIT

CATIMP

HAVEN'T YOU EVER
SEEN THIS?

Now arrange the circled letters to form the
surprise answer, as suggested by the above
cartoon.

Print
answer
here

" A ⬡⬡⬡⬡⬡ ⬡⬡⬡⬡⬡ "

JUMBLE®

Unscramble these four Jumbles, one letter to
each square, to form four ordinary words.

THICY

KAFLE

FELDIE

RUSLAW

AFTER ANOTHER WOM-
AN HAD "TURNED" HIS
HEAD, HE OBVIOUSLY
COULDN'T DO THIS
ANYMORE.

Now arrange the circled letters to form the
surprise answer, as suggested by the above
cartoon.

Print answer here ⬚⬚⬚⬚⬚ HIS ⬚⬚⬚⬚

JUMBLE®

Unscramble these four Jumbles, one letter to each square, to form four ordinary words.

ENVIL

LIDUF

INGINN

FEEDAM

THE DENTIST GREW FAT BECAUSE ALMOST EVERYTHING HE TOUCHED WAS THIS.

Now arrange the circled letters to form the surprise answer, as suggested by the above cartoon.

Print answer here

JUMBLE®

Unscramble these four Jumbles, one letter to each square, to form four ordinary words.

CENUD

DAUGY

TRIVEN

DOLIBY

WHAT DID THE BORED COW SAY WHEN SHE GOT UP IN THE MORNING?

Now arrange the circled letters to form the surprise answer, as suggested by the above cartoon.

Print answer here " JUST AN ⬭⬭⬭⬭⬭ ⬭⬭⬭ "

JUMBLE®

Unscramble these four Jumbles, one letter to each square, to form four ordinary words.

MAGLE

TINGY

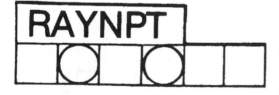

RAYNPT

MESHEC

HOW DOES A BABY CHICK FIT INTO ITS SHELL?

Now arrange the circled letters to form the surprise answer, as suggested by the above cartoon.

Print answer here "  "

JUMBLE®

Unscramble these four Jumbles, one letter to each square, to form four ordinary words.

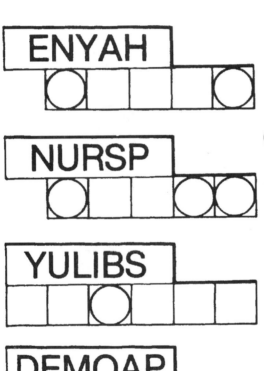

ENYAH

NURSP

YULIBS

DEMOAP

WHAT DO YOU GET WHEN YOU CROSS A CACTUS WITH A PORCUPINE?

Now arrange the circled letters to form the surprise answer, as suggested by the above cartoon.

Print answer here

JUMBLE

Unscramble these four Jumbles, one letter to each square, to form four ordinary words.

NAGET

BLAYK

DANNIL

SEBIED

WHAT BRINGS FLOWERS?

Now arrange the circled letters to form the surprise answer, as suggested by the above cartoon.

Print answer here THE " ⭕⭕⭕⭕⭕ "

9

JUMBLE®

Unscramble these four Jumbles, one letter to
each square, to form four ordinary words.

HISFY

TOTID

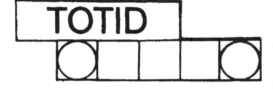

KLINTE

BRYFLE

KIDS' CLOTHES WILL
STAY CLEAN MUCH
LONGER IF YOU
KEEP THEM THIS.

Now arrange the circled letters to form the
surprise answer, as suggested by the above
cartoon.

Print answer here

JUMBLE®

Unscramble these four Jumbles, one letter to each square, to form four ordinary words.

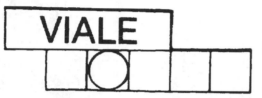

VIALE

ILVIC

THEIRE

AMBALS

WHAT DO LIARS DO AFTER THEY DIE?

Now arrange the circled letters to form the surprise answer, as suggested by the above cartoon.

Print answer here ⬡⬡⬡ ⬡⬡⬡⬡⬡

JUMBLE®

Unscramble these four Jumbles, one letter to each square, to form four ordinary words.

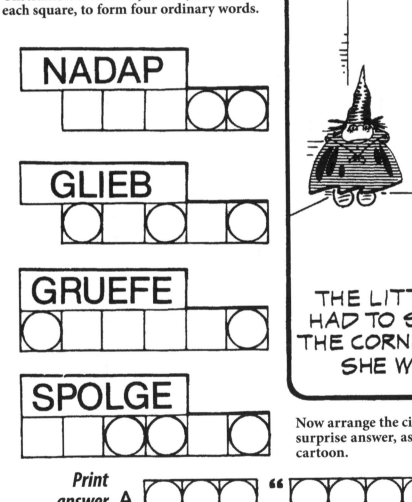

NADAP

GLIEB

GRUEFE

SPOLGE

THE LITTLE WITCH HAD TO STAND IN THE CORNER BECAUSE SHE WAS THIS.

Now arrange the circled letters to form the surprise answer, as suggested by the above cartoon.

Print answer here

A

JUMBLE®

Unscramble these four Jumbles, one letter to
each square, to form four ordinary words.

THOUY

BIGEE

REGAHN

VYCOON

WHAT THE DOCTOR
SAID ABOUT THE CON-
DITION OF THE GUY
WHO HAD SWALLOWED
A HALF-DOLLAR.

Now arrange the circled letters to form the
surprise answer, as suggested by the above
cartoon.

**Print
answer
here**

JUMBLE®

Unscramble these four Jumbles, one letter to
each square, to form four ordinary words.

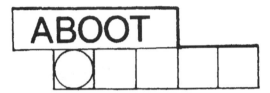

ABOOT

GLAVE

TOYBUN

MADGEA

THE FARMER BECAME
ANGRY WHEN SOME-
ONE MANAGED
TO DO THIS.

Now arrange the circled letters to form the
surprise answer, as suggested by the above
cartoon.

Print answer here  HIS

14

JUMBLE®

Unscramble these four Jumbles, one letter to
each square, to form four ordinary words.

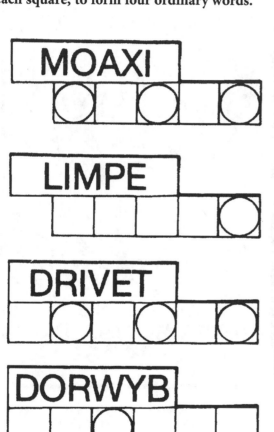

MOAXI

LIMPE

DRIVET

DORWYB

MOM AND DAD WERE
KEPT AWAKE ALL
NIGHT WHILE JUNIOR
WAS HAVING THIS.

Now arrange the circled letters to form the
surprise answer, as suggested by the above
cartoon.

Print answer here A " ⬡⬡⬡⬡ " OF A ⬡⬡⬡⬡

JUMBLE®

Unscramble these four Jumbles, one letter to
each square, to form four ordinary words.

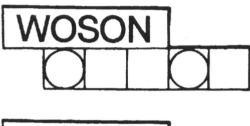

WOSON

RIGMY

TREENI

ANGAME

Some job getting her off our hands!

COULD BE INSTRUMENTAL IN A MARRIAGE.

Now arrange the circled letters to form the
surprise answer, as suggested by the above
cartoon.

Print answer here THE

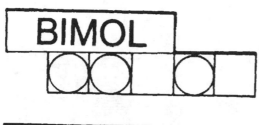

JUMBLE®

Unscramble these four Jumbles, one letter to each square, to form four ordinary words.

BIMOL

HURCS

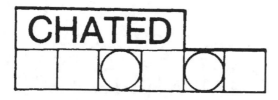

CHATED

GINKAB

WHERE THOSE OLD-TIME WARRIORS WENT ON THEIR EVENINGS OFF.

Now arrange the circled letters to form the surprise answer, as suggested by the above cartoon.

Print answer here TO A "◯◯◯◯◯◯ ◯◯◯◯"

JUMBLE®

Unscramble these four Jumbles, one letter to each square, to form four ordinary words.

YILSK

ENPOY

ENCAME

DEGUMS

WHAT SHOULD A SWORD SWALLOWER EAT WHEN HE'S ON A DIET?

Now arrange the circled letters to form the surprise answer, as suggested by the above cartoon.

Print answer here ☐☐☐☐☐ & ☐☐☐☐☐☐☐☐☐

JUMBLE®

Unscramble these four Jumbles, one letter to
each square, to form four ordinary words.

KESTO

TULDA

CUBLEK

CISEXE

WHAT HAPPENED
TO THE MAN
WHO SUED
THE PORTER?

Now arrange the circled letters to form the
surprise answer, as suggested by the above
cartoon.

Print answer here HE ⬡⬡⬡⬡ HIS ⬡⬡⬡⬡

JUMBLE.

Unscramble these four Jumbles, one letter to each square, to form four ordinary words.

GUZAE

KWISH

UNGOAT

THAGUT

WHAT DO YOU CALL IT WHEN PIGS DO THEIR LAUNDRY?

Now arrange the circled letters to form the surprise answer, as suggested by the above cartoon.

Print answer here

JUMBLE®

Unscramble these four Jumbles, one letter to each square, to form four ordinary words.

KLEAN

TYMPE

VEEBAH

NEAFED

How can I get through all that lard?

THE PATIENTS DIDN'T LIKE THAT NURSE BE- CAUSE SHE WAS AL- WAYS TRYING TO DO THIS.

Now arrange the circled letters to form the surprise answer, as suggested by the above cartoon.

Print answer here

21

JUMBLE®

Unscramble these four Jumbles, one letter to
each square, to form four ordinary words.

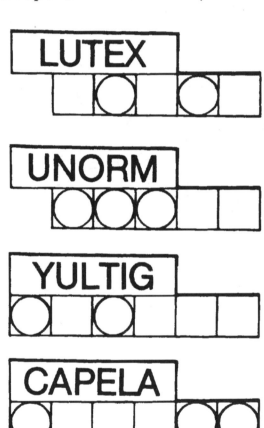

LUTEX

UNORM

YULTIG

CAPELA

WHAT TEQUILA IS.

Now arrange the circled letters to form the
surprise answer, as suggested by the above
cartoon.

Print
answer THE "◯◯◯◯" OF ◯◯◯◯◯◯◯
here

JUMBLE®

Unscramble these four Jumbles, one letter to
each square, to form four ordinary words.

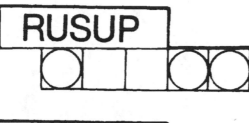

RUSUP

FONTE

PECTOK

ENLOOD

IF YOU WANT TO
BUY A GOOD WIG,
YOU SURE
HAVE THIS.

Now arrange the circled letters to form the
surprise answer, as suggested by the above
cartoon.

Print answer here  IT

JUMBLE®

Unscramble these four Jumbles, one letter to each square, to form four ordinary words.

TUBOA
◻⭕◻◻⭕

NIDEK
⭕◻⭕◻◻

DOBOLY
◻⭕◻⭕◻◻

HINEAL
⭕◻◻◻⭕⭕

WHAT'S WRONG WITH EATING THIS LITTLE OL' APPLE?

Now arrange the circled letters to form the surprise answer, as suggested by the above cartoon.

Print answer here " ◻. ◻. , ◻'◻◻ ◻◻◻◻ "

JUMBLE®

Unscramble these four Jumbles, one letter to each square, to form four ordinary words.

ATAGE

NOPER

CRYLEE

NEPAHP

WHY NEXT YEAR
IS A GOOD YEAR
FOR KANGAROOS.

Now arrange the circled letters to form the surprise answer, as suggested by the above cartoon.

Print answer here IT'S "⬡⬡⬡⬡" ⬡⬡⬡⬡

JUMBLE®

Unscramble these four Jumbles, one letter to each square, to form four ordinary words.

DEWPI

TALAN

NEPTLY

ERRTAY

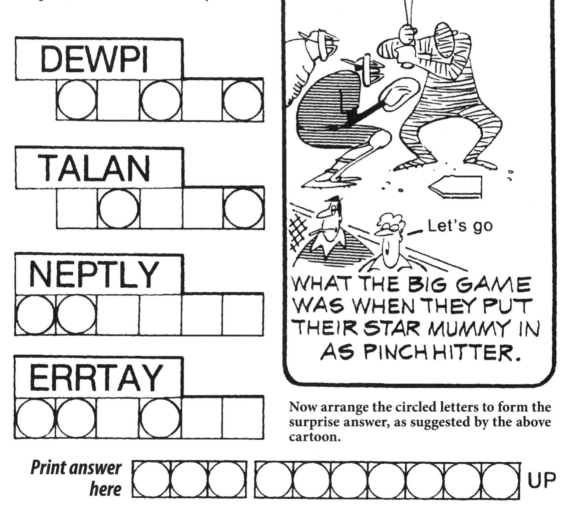

Let's go

WHAT THE BIG GAME WAS WHEN THEY PUT THEIR STAR MUMMY IN AS PINCH HITTER.

Now arrange the circled letters to form the surprise answer, as suggested by the above cartoon.

Print answer here ⬚⬚⬚ ⬚⬚⬚⬚⬚⬚⬚ UP

JUMBLE®

Unscramble these four Jumbles, one letter to each square, to form four ordinary words.

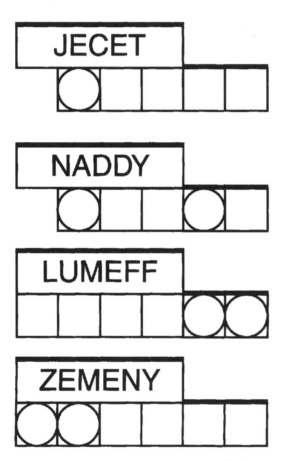

JECET

NADDY

LUMEFF

ZEMENY

Oh, my

Maybe he'll grow into it

WHAT THE KNITTERS DID WHEN SHE MADE THE SLEEVE TOO LONG.

Now arrange the circled letters to form the surprise answer, as suggested by the above cartoon.

Print answer here  **HER**

JUMBLE®

Unscramble these four Jumbles, one letter to each square, to form four ordinary words.

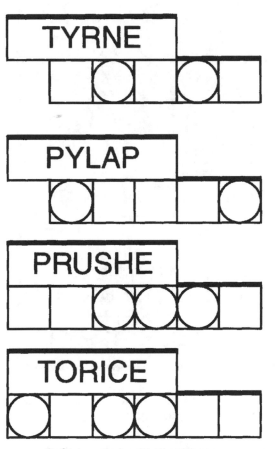

TYRNE

PYLAP

PRUSHE

TORICE

That #$%&* rock!

$#%*%!!

THAT GARDENER WAS KNOWN FOR REMARKS LIKE THIS.

Now arrange the circled letters to form the surprise answer, as suggested by the above cartoon.

Print answer here

" ⬡⬡⬡⬡⬡⬡ " ⬡⬡⬡⬡

29

JUMBLE®

Unscramble these four Jumbles, one letter to each square, to form four ordinary words.

VACHO

THECK

GILOOG

SUMOTT

He didn't feel a thing

WHAT THE ELECTRICIAN-TURNED-PICKPOCKET HAD.

Now arrange the circled letters to form the surprise answer, as suggested by the above cartoon.

Print answer here A " ⬡⬡⬡⬡⬡ " ⬡⬡⬡⬡⬡

JUMBLE®

Unscramble these four Jumbles, one letter to
each square, to form four ordinary words.

CHITH

MUBIE

CORLLS

OOLANG

My nurse will
give him a shot

And I'll
give him
an aspirin

RARELY PER-
FORMED
BY A DOCTOR.

Now arrange the circled letters to form the
surprise answer, as suggested by the above
cartoon.

Print
answer A
here

JUMBLE®

Unscramble these four Jumbles, one letter to each square, to form four ordinary words.

ARBOX

DAGLE

UNJORI

DUNJOC

See? Nothing to it

SHE SAID THIS
WHEN HUBBY
MENDED HIS SOCK.

Now arrange the circled letters to form the surprise answer, as suggested by the above cartoon.

Print answer here

" ⃝⃝⃝⃝ " ⃝⃝⃝⃝⃝ ⃝⃝⃝⃝

JUMBLE®

Unscramble these four Jumbles, one letter to each square, to form four ordinary words.

FLUTA

ALOCK

ETTIPE

REPUMB

WHAT THEY CALLED THAT COMICAL SURGEON.

Now arrange the circled letters to form the surprise answer, as suggested by the above cartoon.

Print answer here A

JUMBLE®

Unscramble these four Jumbles, one letter to each square, to form four ordinary words.

SHYKU

MUSIN

WAIRND

BALEEG

He's so cute

I'll introduce you

SHE WANTED TO MEET THE SPRINTER BECAUSE HE WAS ----

Now arrange the circled letters to form the surprise answer, as suggested by the above cartoon.

Print answer here

JUMBLE®

Unscramble these four Jumbles, one letter to each square, to form four ordinary words.

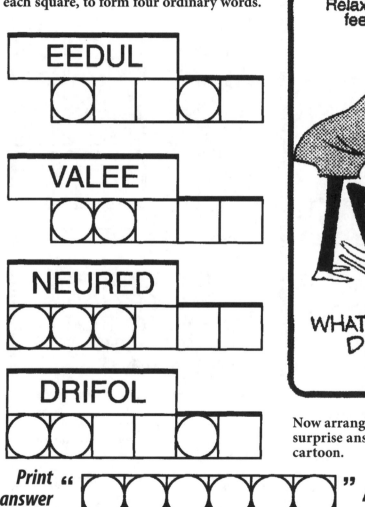

EEDUL

VALEE

NEURED

DRIFOL

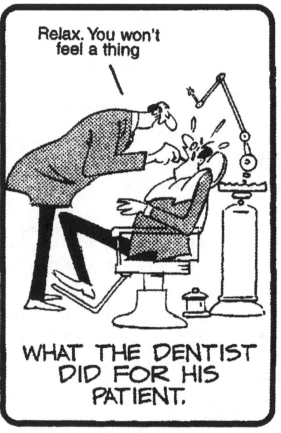

Relax. You won't feel a thing

WHAT THE DENTIST DID FOR HIS PATIENT.

Now arrange the circled letters to form the surprise answer, as suggested by the above cartoon.

Print **"** ⬡⬡⬡⬡⬡⬡ **" A** ⬡⬡⬡⬡
answer
here

JUMBLE®

Unscramble these four Jumbles, one letter to
each square, to form four ordinary words.

LUSKK

LERIN

FLUGAR

RANLYX

THE GEOMETRY
TEACHER WAS
TOUGH TO FOOL
BECAUSE
SHE KNEW ——

Now arrange the circled letters to form the
surprise answer, as suggested by the above
cartoon.

Print answer here ⬡⬡⬡ **THE** ⬡⬡⬡⬡⬡⬡⬡

JUMBLE®

Unscramble these four Jumbles, one letter to
each square, to form four ordinary words.

KEVOE

DONSY

COBNEK

COBEME

How about a big, juicy steak
while you check my records?

WHAT THE SHADY
RESTAURANT
OWNER DID FOR
THE TAX
COLLECTOR.

Now arrange the circled letters to form the
surprise answer, as suggested by the above
cartoon.

Print
answer
here ⬡⬡⬡⬡⬡ THE ⬡⬡⬡⬡⬡

JUMBLE

Unscramble these four Jumbles, one letter to each square, to form four ordinary words.

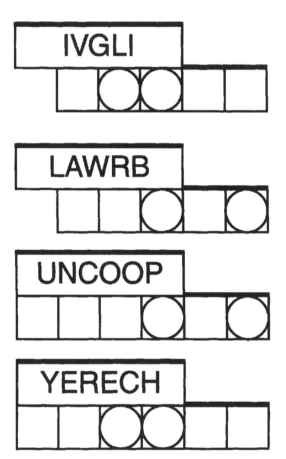

IVGLI

LAWRB

UNCOOP

YERECH

Tastes great

And easy to eat

THE KIDS LIKED BANANAS BECAUSE THEY WERE —

Now arrange the circled letters to form the surprise answer, as suggested by the above cartoon.

Print answer here "◯ - ◯◯◯◯◯◯◯"

38

JUMBLE®

Unscramble these four Jumbles, one letter to each square, to form four ordinary words.

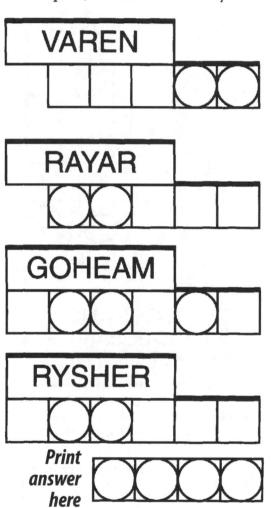

VAREN

RAYAR

GOHEAM

RYSHER

He's good

He practically lives here

WHAT DAILY TARGET PRACTICE MADE HIM FEEL LIKE.

Now arrange the circled letters to form the surprise answer, as suggested by the above cartoon.

Print answer here ◯◯◯◯ ON THE ◯◯◯◯◯

JUMBLE®

Unscramble these four Jumbles, one letter to
each square, to form four ordinary words.

UPMEL

BAWLY

NESCHO

CHECIT

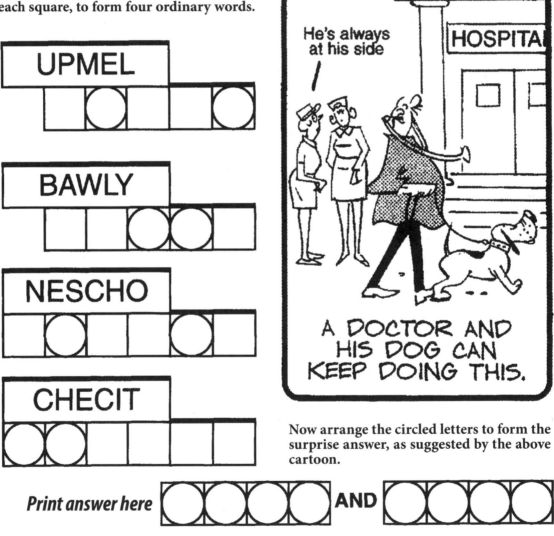

He's always
at his side

HOSPITAL

A DOCTOR AND
HIS DOG CAN
KEEP DOING THIS.

Now arrange the circled letters to form the
surprise answer, as suggested by the above
cartoon.

Print answer here ⬡⬡⬡⬡ AND ⬡⬡⬡⬡

JUMBLE®

Unscramble these four Jumbles, one letter to each square, to form four ordinary words.

SURNP

HOLEL

MASTIG

LETLIF

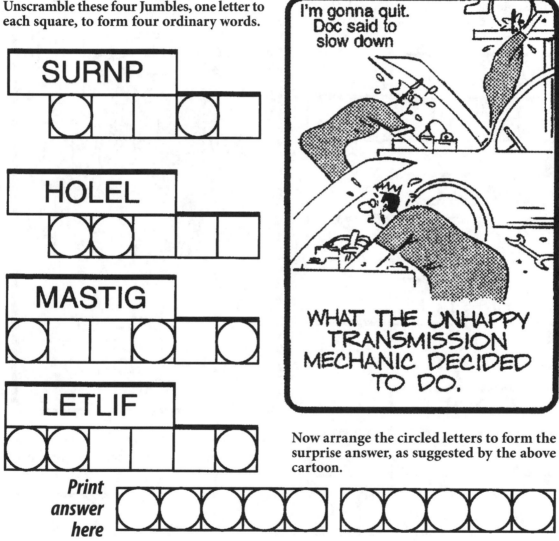

I'm gonna quit. Doc said to slow down

WHAT THE UNHAPPY TRANSMISSION MECHANIC DECIDED TO DO.

Now arrange the circled letters to form the surprise answer, as suggested by the above cartoon.

Print answer here

JUMBLE®

Unscramble these four Jumbles, one letter to each square, to form four ordinary words.

CAZER

BREWO

WHARTT

MODDEO

Looks just like her

PORTRAITS
$2.50

THE STREET ARTIST LIKED TO DO THIS.

Now arrange the circled letters to form the surprise answer, as suggested by the above cartoon.

Print answer here "〇〇〇〇" A 〇〇〇〇〇

JUMBLE®

Unscramble these four Jumbles, one letter to each square, to form four ordinary words.

REMEB

RIDAC

CRASAF

RAMAAD

What time is it when both hands are on twelve?

WHAT THE CLOWN DID AT THE CLOCK FACTORY.

Now arrange the circled letters to form the surprise answer, as suggested by the above cartoon.

Print answer here

JUMBLE®

Unscramble these four Jumbles, one letter to
each square, to form four ordinary words.

MEWNO

PROWE

BOSULE

WYSORD

Three
more
times
today

Tough
job

Some
days
are better
than others

A FIREMAN'S JOB
HAS THIS.

Now arrange the circled letters to form the
surprise answer, as suggested by the above
cartoon.

*Print
answer
here* ITS ◯◯◯ AND ◯◯◯◯◯

JUMBLE®

Unscramble these four Jumbles, one letter to each square, to form four ordinary words.

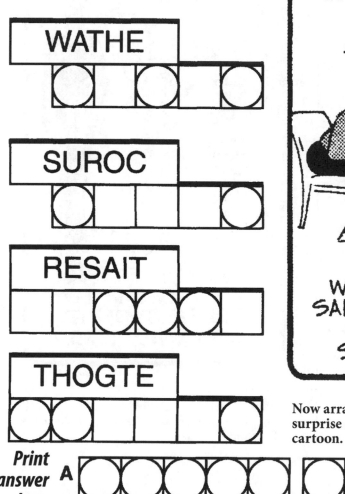

WATHE

SUROC

RESAIT

THOGTE

... and then they heard a creaky door open ...

WHAT THE KIDS SAID THE AUTHOR OF SPOOKY STORIES WAS.

Now arrange the circled letters to form the surprise answer, as suggested by the above cartoon.

Print answer here   A ⬚⬚⬚⬚⬚   ⬚⬚⬚⬚⬚⬚

JUMBLE®

Unscramble these four Jumbles, one letter to each square, to form four ordinary words.

AVVLE

NICEW

DARZIL

BOWELL

Perfect! My compliments to the chef

WHEN A STEAK IS COOKED TO PERFECTION IT BECOMES THIS.

Now arrange the circled letters to form the surprise answer, as suggested by the above cartoon.

Print answer here

JUMBLE®

Unscramble these four Jumbles, one letter to each square, to form four ordinary words.

OMSKY

CHALT

YATAPH

LINKUE

Ugh, what a job

IT TAKES THIS TO FEATHER A CHICKEN.

Now arrange the circled letters to form the surprise answer, as suggested by the above cartoon.

Print answer here [ ][ ][ ][ ] OF [ ][ ][ ][ ][ ]

JUMBLE®

Unscramble these four Jumbles, one letter to
each square, to form four ordinary words.

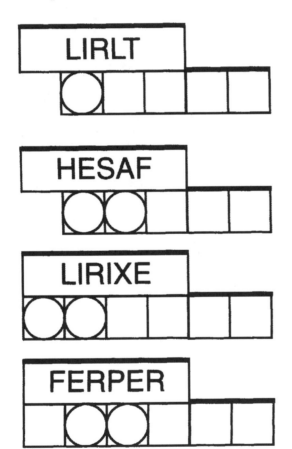

LIRLT

HESAF

LIRIXE

FERPER

You need
some tax
write offs

Wait, I need
an umbrella

UMBRELLA
SALE

WHAT THE
INVESTOR WANTED
FOR A RAINY DAY.

Now arrange the circled letters to form the
surprise answer, as suggested by the above
cartoon.

Print answer here **A**

JUMBLE®

Unscramble these four Jumbles, one letter to
each square, to form four ordinary words.

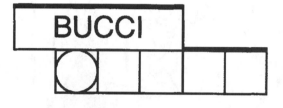

BUCCI

DRAIP

CLAARN

MENUBB

That must
be tough work

I doubled my
pay, 4 weeks
vacation, and ...

WHY HE TOOK
THE DIRTY JOB.

Now arrange the circled letters to form the
surprise answer, as suggested by the above
cartoon.

Print answer here   TO

49

JUMBLE®

Unscramble these four Jumbles, one letter to each square, to form four ordinary words.

ZALBE

MAGEL

SCUMEL

TROPSY

Now arrange the circled letters to form the surprise answer, as suggested by the above cartoon.

Print answer here A "◯◯◯◯◯◯◯" ◯◯◯

JUMBLE®

Unscramble these four Jumbles, one letter to each square, to form four ordinary words.

HILEW

GEALE

LIRMAN

NAWKEE

This is perfect

It's my secret process

INTRODUCED BY THE DRY CLEANER TO INCREASE BUSINESS.

Now arrange the circled letters to form the surprise answer, as suggested by the above cartoon.

Print answer here

A

51

JUMBLE®

Unscramble these four Jumbles, one letter to each square, to form four ordinary words.

CRAHN

CUMSI

KLARTE

TORTOG

Congratulations

Always courteous and prompt

THE CONDUCTOR WAS PROMOTED BECAUSE HE WAS ----

Now arrange the circled letters to form the surprise answer, as suggested by the above cartoon.

Print answer here **ON THE** ◯◯◯◯◯ " ◯◯◯◯◯ "

JUMBLE®

Unscramble these four Jumbles, one letter to
each square, to form four ordinary words.

PYKER

UMBOX

MOVULE

MEAFED

I clean while you just
sit there. GET OUT!

Shh, I'm
thinking

WHAT THE UN-
HAPPY ROOMMATE
FORCED THE
CHESS WHIZ
TO DO.

Now arrange the circled letters to form the
surprise answer, as suggested by the above
cartoon.

Print answer here ⬭⬭⬭⬭ A ⬭⬭⬭⬭

JUMBLE®

Unscramble these four Jumbles, one letter to each square, to form four ordinary words.

CAMIG

NINOO

GAYMIB

BOLUDE

Mom, you've got E-mail

WHAT THE COMPUTER OPERATOR ENDED UP DOING ON HER DAY OFF.

Now arrange the circled letters to form the surprise answer, as suggested by the above cartoon.

Print answer here ⬡⬡⬡⬡⬡ ON ⬡⬡⬡⬡

JUMBLE®

Unscramble these four Jumbles, one letter to each square, to form four ordinary words.

YOLID

KNUSK

SIMFLY

GRATUI

This is awful

I can't take a breath

HOW THE DUMP LEFT THE NEIGHBORS.

Now arrange the circled letters to form the surprise answer, as suggested by the above cartoon.

Print answer here

JUMBLE®

Unscramble these four Jumbles, one letter to
each square, to form four ordinary words.

LIDAP

YORFT

EXPLUD

BUHSIL

Don't forget your woolies

Do you miss me, Harold?

Fido, don't chase the cats

WHAT THE
SÉANCE BECAME.

Now arrange the circled letters to form the
surprise answer, as suggested by the above
cartoon.

Print answer here

JUMBLE®

Unscramble these four Jumbles, one letter to each square, to form four ordinary words.

NUMOR

SINEA

HESTOO

YELMOP

You're in perfect shape

Who are you kidding?!

THIS WILL MAKE A HYPOCHONDRIAC SICK.

Now arrange the circled letters to form the surprise answer, as suggested by the above cartoon.

Print answer here

JUMBLE®

Unscramble these four Jumbles, one letter to each square, to form four ordinary words.

TEAHB

TUINY

YETLEE

PRIMEE

Congratulations, you broke my strikeout record

WHAT THE STUDENTS CALLED THE MAIL CARRIER AND THE ATHLETE.

Now arrange the circled letters to form the surprise answer, as suggested by the above cartoon.

Print answer here

JUMBLE®

Unscramble these four Jumbles, one letter to each square, to form four ordinary words.

NUTED

RAPEP

WECHEN

BELUCK

Thanks, fellas

He won every hand

WHAT THE JANITOR DID DURING HIS LUNCH BREAK.

Now arrange the circled letters to form the surprise answer, as suggested by the above cartoon.

Print answer here

JUMBLE®

Unscramble these four Jumbles, one letter to each square, to form four ordinary words.

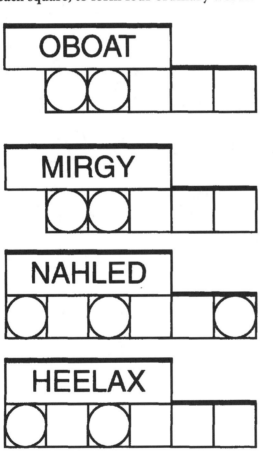

OBOAT

MIRGY

NAHLED

HEELAX

How long will I be here?

Patience

IMPORTANT TO DO AFTER A SKIING ACCIDENT.

Now arrange the circled letters to form the surprise answer, as suggested by the above cartoon.

Print answer here

IN

JUMBLE®

Unscramble these four Jumbles, one letter to
each square, to form four ordinary words.

ADDIE
◯◯

NITLE
◯◯◯

STEEWF
◯◯◯

BALIVE
◯◯◯

I wore this
for years

You're
choking
me!

WHAT DAD'S OLD
SCHOOL
NECKWEAR
BECAME.

Now arrange the circled letters to form the
surprise answer, as suggested by the above
cartoon.

*Print
answer
here* THE ◯◯◯ THAT ◯◯◯◯◯

JUMBLE®

Unscramble these four Jumbles, one letter to
each square, to form four ordinary words.

KYACT

FITAH

CUNESS

CLAFIA

Wow! He just
missed the wall

WHOOSH!!

A SUCCESSFUL
RACE CAR DRIVER
DOES THIS.

Now arrange the circled letters to form the
surprise answer, as suggested by the above
cartoon.

*Print
answer
here* ◯◯◯◯◯◯ "◯◯◯◯"

JUMBLE®

Unscramble these four Jumbles, one letter to each square, to form four ordinary words.

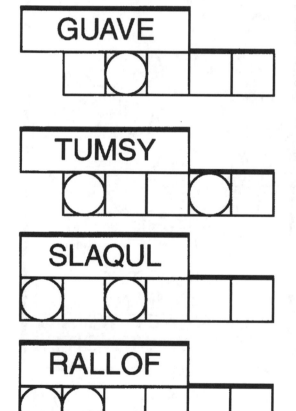

GUAVE

TUMSY

SLAQUL

RALLOF

That's all I've got

THE SECURITY DEPOSIT ON THE APARTMENT AMOUNTED TO THIS.

Now arrange the circled letters to form the surprise answer, as suggested by the above cartoon.

Print answer here **A** " ◯◯◯◯ " ◯◯◯

JUMBLE®

Unscramble these four Jumbles, one letter to
each square, to form four ordinary words.

ALLAM

SLEBS

HEBLED

TURAIN

There's a good offer

I never heard of
them before

WHAT THE
COMPANY
IMPROVED WITH
ITS NEW WEB SITE.

Now arrange the circled letters to form the
surprise answer, as suggested by the above
cartoon.

Print answer here " ___ " ___

JUMBLE®

Unscramble these four Jumbles, one letter to each square, to form four ordinary words.

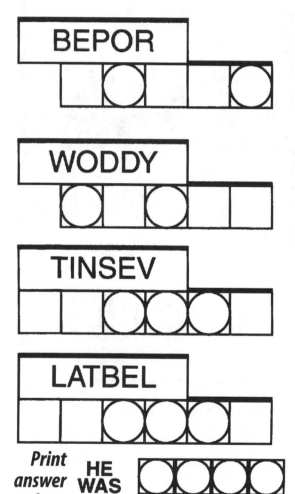

BEPOR

WODDY

TINSEV

LATBEL

... and his sinewy mass of masculinity ...

He's wonderful

A walking dictionary

WHY THEY LISTENED TO HIS POETRY.

Now arrange the circled letters to form the surprise answer, as suggested by the above cartoon.

Print answer here   HE WAS

"⬭⬭⬭⬭⬭⬭⬭"

JUMBLE®

Unscramble these four Jumbles, one letter to each square, to form four ordinary words.

SIPOE

THRIM

DIPALL

CLUGED

That's it, keep pedaling

WHAT THE DIVORCE JUDGE GAVE HIS SON.

Now arrange the circled letters to form the surprise answer, as suggested by the above cartoon.

Print answer here

JUMBLE®

Unscramble these four Jumbles, one letter to each square, to form four ordinary words.

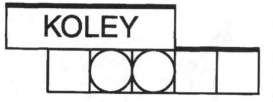

KOLEY

PIGER

HOYLUR

CROOPE

I could do this all day

EASY TO TURN INTO AT A VACATION LODGE.

Now arrange the circled letters to form the surprise answer, as suggested by the above cartoon.

Print answer here A "◯◯◯◯◯" ◯◯◯◯◯◯

JUMBLE®

Unscramble these four Jumbles, one letter to
each square, to form four ordinary words.

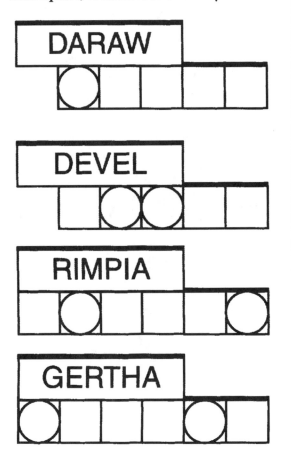

DARAW

DEVEL

RIMPIA

GERTHA

Smedley, you
do nice work

WHAT THE
JEWELER
CONSIDERED HIS
HARD-WORKING
CLERK.

Now arrange the circled letters to form the
surprise answer, as suggested by the above
cartoon.

 **Print answer here** **A**

JUMBLE®

Unscramble these four Jumbles, one letter to each square, to form four ordinary words.

GUBEN

SUGIE

TAUNER

CASTUC

The answer is, "Who go there?"

No-no-no ... It's "Who GOES there?"

AN UPTIGHT GRAMMARIAN IS ALWAYS THIS.

Now arrange the circled letters to form the surprise answer, as suggested by the above cartoon.

Print answer here " "

JUMBLE®

Unscramble these four Jumbles, one letter to
each square, to form four ordinary words.

PORDO

RALNS

PREDON

LAMDAY

WHAT THE
WOULD-BE DIVA
TURNED LAUNDRY
DAY INTO.

Now arrange the circled letters to form the
surprise answer, as suggested by the above
cartoon.

Print answer here **A**

JUMBLE®

Unscramble these four Jumbles, one letter to
each square, to form four ordinary words.

CASEE

WHEGI

RAWHEL

THACED

C'mon, lady, I
ain't got all day

WHY SHE DISLIKED
THE NASTY SHOE
SALESMAN.

Now arrange the circled letters to form the
surprise answer, as suggested by the above
cartoon.

Print answer here ⬜⬜ ⬜⬜⬜ A ⬜⬜⬜⬜

JUMBLE®

Unscramble these four Jumbles, one letter to
each square, to form four ordinary words.

OTHIS

NILAF

BRYFLE

CLOPEM

I'll take two

They're
going like
hot cakes

50%
OFF
SALE

WHAT THE
MERCHANT
REALIZED WHEN
THE NEGLIGEES
WENT ON SALE.

Now arrange the circled letters to form the
surprise answer, as suggested by the above
cartoon.

**Print
answer A
here**

" ⬡⬡⬡⬡⬡⬡ " ⬡⬡⬡⬡⬡⬡

JUMBLE.

Unscramble these four Jumbles, one letter to each square, to form four ordinary words.

BOYHB

BIBER

CORTER

PASHIM

Do you take credit cards?

HE RACED FOR THE TRAIN AND ENDED UP SHORT OF THIS.

Now arrange the circled letters to form the surprise answer, as suggested by the above cartoon.

Print answer here

JUMBLE®

Unscramble these four Jumbles, one letter to each square, to form four ordinary words.

BROAN

BIATH

CUGHAT

ROESIE

Someone always takes it for the summer

WHY HE NEVER WORRIED ABOUT RENTING THE BEACH HOUSE.

Now arrange the circled letters to form the surprise answer, as suggested by the above cartoon.

Print answer here   IT WAS A ☐☐☐☐☐ ☐☐☐☐☐

JUMBLE®

Unscramble these four Jumbles, one letter to each square, to form four ordinary words.

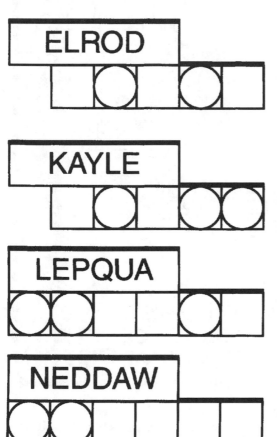

ELROD

KAYLE

LEPQUA

NEDDAW

Relax

BEFORE THE CONCERT THE PIANIST WAS ---

Now arrange the circled letters to form the surprise answer, as suggested by the above cartoon.

Print answer here

JUMBLE®

Unscramble these four Jumbles, one letter to
each square, to form four ordinary words.

GINIC

HECAF

RAHBOR

FLARTE

Are you sure it works?

It cuts my
appetite

DID SHE LOSE
WEIGHT ON THE
ICE CREAM DIET?

Now arrange the circled letters to form the
surprise answer, as suggested by the above
cartoon.

Print answer here

JUMBLE®

Unscramble these four Jumbles, one letter to each square, to form four ordinary words.

LODDY

DARAM

DINNAL

BOUGER

I hope I never see you again!

It's about time you paid

WHAT THE BILL COLLECTOR GOT WHEN THE DEBT WAS FINALLY PAID.

Now arrange the circled letters to form the surprise answer, as suggested by the above cartoon.

Print answer here **A** " ⬡⬡⬡ " ⬡⬡⬡⬡

JUMBLE®

Unscramble these four Jumbles, one letter to each square, to form four ordinary words.

KROJE

YONOL

TAPCER

MALLYC

Who did this?

WHAT MOM WANTED
THE KIDS TO DO
WHEN THE HOUSE
WAS A MESS.

Now arrange the circled letters to form the surprise answer, as suggested by the above cartoon.

Print answer here

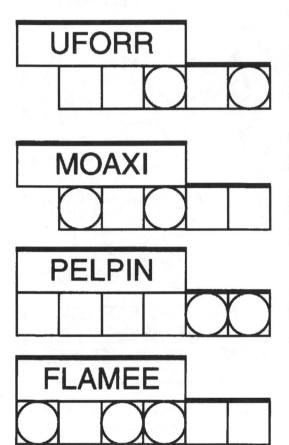

JUMBLE®

Unscramble these four Jumbles, one letter to
each square, to form four ordinary words.

UFORR

MOAXI

PELPIN

FLAMEE

I hear four people
are going

Oh no, I
just bought
a new car

LAYOFF RUMORS
CAN SET THIS OFF.

Now arrange the circled letters to form the
surprise answer, as suggested by the above
cartoon.

Print
answer
here

A " ◯◯◯◯ " ◯◯◯◯◯◯

JUMBLE®

Unscramble these four Jumbles, one letter to
each square, to form four ordinary words.

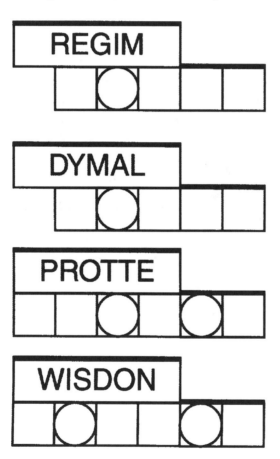

REGIM

DYMAL

PROTTE

WISDON

Where are
my meals?

Patience, I'm
swamped

WHAT THE SERVER
BECAME WHEN THE
COOK FELL BEHIND.

Now arrange the circled letters to form the
surprise answer, as suggested by the above
cartoon.

Print answer here **A**

JUMBLE®

Unscramble these four Jumbles, one letter to
each square, to form four ordinary words.

TUXEL

SUMEO

CHARNB

SWETID

For
me?

SHE GOT CANDY
BECAUSE HE WAS ----

Now arrange the circled letters to form the
surprise answer, as suggested by the above
cartoon.

Print answer here ⬡⬡⬡⬡⬡ **ON** ⬡⬡⬡

JUMBLE®

Unscramble these four Jumbles, one letter to
each square, to form four ordinary words.

ZALEH

DDAYD

BEHREY

BLIMER

Two million
a year

Nothing less
than three

THE BATTING
STAR GOT THE
BIG CONTRACT
BY PLAYING ——

Now arrange the circled letters to form the
surprise answer, as suggested by the above
cartoon.

Print answer here " ◯◯◯◯◯◯◯◯ "

JUMBLE®

Unscramble these four Jumbles, one letter to each square, to form four ordinary words.

PUDMY

WONGI

TIMOON

PELSOG

You'll be fine, but I have to admit you

WHERE THE INJURED LUMBERJACK ENDED UP AFTER TREATMENT.

Now arrange the circled letters to form the surprise answer, as suggested by the above cartoon.

Print answer here ◯◯◯ **OF THE** ◯◯◯◯◯

JUMBLE®

Unscramble these four Jumbles, one letter to each square, to form four ordinary words.

FLEAY

EUQUE

PALLAP

CROVAT

I can promise you a big return

He looks honest, let's invest

WHAT THE STOCK-BROKER INCREASED WITH A SMILE.

Now arrange the circled letters to form the surprise answer, as suggested by the above cartoon.

Print answer here HIS ⬜⬜⬜⬜ ⬜⬜⬜⬜⬜

JUMBLE®

Unscramble these four Jumbles, one letter to
each square, to form four ordinary words.

WEHIN

YOANG

AREPPA

TULYSS

You have young eyes

You don't look thirty

WHY THE PHONE OPERATOR DREADED THE BIRTHDAY BASH.

Now arrange the circled letters to form the
surprise answer, as suggested by the above
cartoon.

Print answer here " "

JUMBLE®

Unscramble these four Jumbles, one letter to each square, to form four ordinary words.

RAAMO

CAROK

DEKOOH

THINEW

We're hungry. When's dinner?

When Dad arrives

WHAT THE TEACHER DID AFTER SCHOOL.

Now arrange the circled letters to form the surprise answer, as suggested by the above cartoon.

Print answer here [ ][ ][ ][ ] [ ][ ][ ][ ]

JUMBLE®

Unscramble these four Jumbles, one letter to
each square, to form four ordinary words.

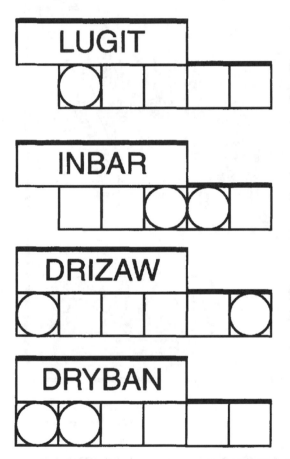

LUGIT

INBAR

DRIZAW

DRYBAN

THE HUGE
MURAL WAS ——

Now arrange the circled letters to form the
surprise answer, as suggested by the above
cartoon.

Print answer here A ◯◯◯ " ◯◯◯◯ "

JUMBLE®

Unscramble these four Jumbles, one letter to
each square, to form four ordinary words.

GEDEH

GHILT

INTEWG

YESWIL

WHAT A LOT OF
FOULS CAN DO TO
A BASKETBALL
REFEREE.

Now arrange the circled letters to form the
surprise answer, as suggested by the above
cartoon.

Print
answer
here   ◯◯◯◯◯ HIS ◯◯◯◯◯◯◯◯

JUMBLE®

Unscramble these four Jumbles, one letter to
each square, to form four ordinary words.

BLEEL

MEFAD

PHUDEL

DENAIG

MOVE! Boy,
you're stubborn

WHY THE FARMER
YELLED AT
THE SOW.

Now arrange the circled letters to form the
surprise answer, as suggested by the above
cartoon.

Print
answer
here   SHE WAS ⬡⬡⬡⬡⬡⬡⬡⬡⬡

JUMBLE®

Unscramble these four Jumbles, one letter to each square, to form four ordinary words.

BEDRY

TAREF

DACARE

ABBOMO

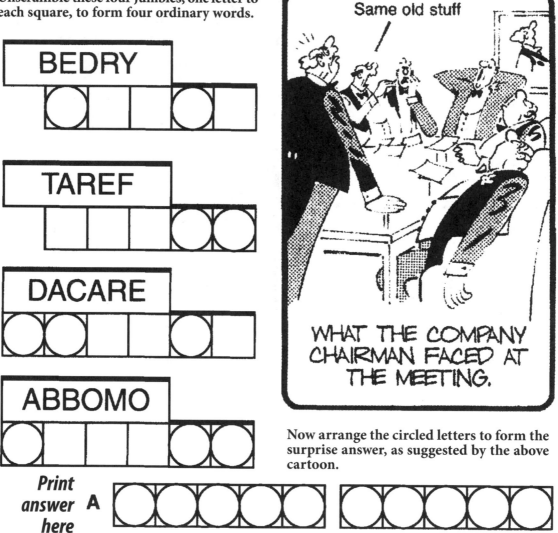

Same old stuff

WHAT THE COMPANY CHAIRMAN FACED AT THE MEETING.

Now arrange the circled letters to form the surprise answer, as suggested by the above cartoon.

Print answer here

A

JUMBLE®

Unscramble these four Jumbles, one letter to
each square, to form four ordinary words.

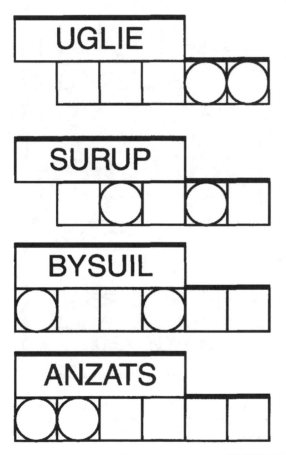

UGLIE

SURUP

BYSUIL

ANZATS

I should have worn gloves

EASY TO RAISE
AFTER THE GARDEN
IS READIED.

Now arrange the circled letters to form the
surprise answer, as suggested by the above
cartoon.

Print answer here

JUMBLE®

Unscramble these four Jumbles, one letter to each square, to form four ordinary words.

PUJMY

SEERA

HOCCUR

NAFELL

Buy Acme stock

Thanks for the tip

WHAT THE BARBER EXPERIENCED WHILE HE WORKED.

Now arrange the circled letters to form the surprise answer, as suggested by the above cartoon.

Print answer here " ◯◯◯◯◯ " ◯◯◯

JUMBLE®

Unscramble these four Jumbles, one letter to
each square, to form four ordinary words.

HOTOB

PRIPE

TONOCY

DEMUGS

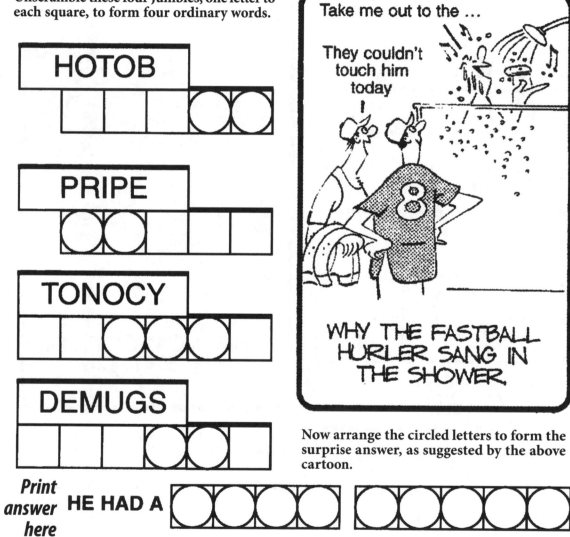

Take me out to the ...

They couldn't
touch him
today

WHY THE FASTBALL
HURLER SANG IN
THE SHOWER.

Now arrange the circled letters to form the
surprise answer, as suggested by the above
cartoon.

**Print
answer
here**   HE HAD A

JUMBLE®

Unscramble these four Jumbles, one letter to
each square, to form four ordinary words.

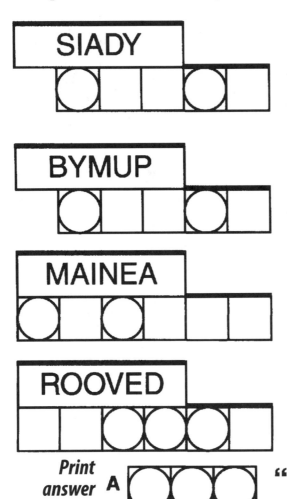

SIADY

BYMUP

MAINEA

ROOVED

WHAT MOM GOT ON
HER BIRTHDAY.

Now arrange the circled letters to form the
surprise answer, as suggested by the above
cartoon.

**Print
answer
here** A ⬜ " ⬜ "

JUMBLE®

Unscramble these four Jumbles, one letter to each square, to form four ordinary words.

EIDUG

MIDIO

FRAGEO

ALUCTA

You keep it in your pocket?

WHEN HE SAW GRANDPA'S WATCH HE THOUGHT IT WAS ----

Now arrange the circled letters to form the surprise answer, as suggested by the above cartoon.

Print answer here AN ◯◯◯ " ◯◯◯◯◯ "

JUMBLE®

Unscramble these four Jumbles, one letter to each square, to form four ordinary words.

JOUMB

CROWE

EVERRE

ROHORR

I can't get the hang of this

WHAT THE BEGINNER ENDED UP KNITTING.

Now arrange the circled letters to form the surprise answer, as suggested by the above cartoon.

Print answer here

JUMBLE®

Unscramble these four Jumbles, one letter to
each square, to form four ordinary words.

MOTEC

HOVUC

TOESGO

DIPAUN

He has the experience

HOW THE BALDING
POLITICIAN FARED
AGAINST THE YOUNG
CANDIDATE.

Now arrange the circled letters to form the
surprise answer, as suggested by the above
cartoon.

Print
answer   HE ⬡⬡⬡⬡ ⬡⬡⬡ ON "⬡⬡⬡"
here

JUMBLE®

Unscramble these four Jumbles, one letter to each square, to form four ordinary words.

STOFI

KANET

TENDAL

CENNAD

Now type in www ...

First I have to sign on

ALWAYS INVOLVED IN AN INTERNET TRANSACTION.

Now arrange the circled letters to form the surprise answer, as suggested by the above cartoon.

Print answer here   THE "⬡⬡⬡⬡⬡⬡" ⬡⬡⬡⬡

JUMBLE®

Unscramble these four Jumbles, one letter to each square, to form four ordinary words.

JARAH

ARVEG

UPCATE

LURTIA

Have a taste, Doc

Give me a pound

SMOKED HAM- 20% OFF

WHAT THE DOCTOR FOUND AT THE MEAT COUNTER.

Now arrange the circled letters to form the surprise answer, as suggested by the above cartoon.

Print answer here

THE ⬡⬡⬡⬡⬡ " ⬡⬡⬡⬡ "

99

JUMBLE®

Unscramble these four Jumbles, one letter to
each square, to form four ordinary words.

TALEE

KERAM

YONNEA

DELDUP

We're ready

This new look takes time

WHAT THE EX-COVER GIRL DID WHEN SHE RESUMED HER CAREER.

Now arrange the circled letters to form the
surprise answer, as suggested by the above
cartoon.

Print answer here ◯◯ - ◯◯◯◯◯◯◯

JUMBLE®

Unscramble these four Jumbles, one letter to
each square, to form four ordinary words.

LANUN

HOPNY

ZENFRY

TOYBAN

Haven't got time for dinner

We leave in
ten minutes

WHEN THE BUSY
PILOT ATE.

Now arrange the circled letters to form the
surprise answer, as suggested by the above
cartoon.

Print answer here ◯◯ ◯◯◯ ◯◯◯

JUMBLE®

Unscramble these four Jumbles, one letter to
each square, to form four ordinary words.

TUNDA

KULFE

WUTTIO

INVOCE

Let's get ready
for another run

WHAT THE
CAREFUL SKI
BOAT OPERATOR
DID.

Now arrange the circled letters to form the
surprise answer, as suggested by the above
cartoon.

*Print answer
here* ◯◯◯◯◯ **THE** ◯◯◯◯

JUMBLE®

Unscramble these four Jumbles, one letter to each square, to form four ordinary words.

INFEG

BELLI

THELME

PERTIL

ANOTHER NAME FOR EVENING HOURS.

Now arrange the circled letters to form the surprise answer, as suggested by the above cartoon.

Print answer " ◯◯◯◯◯ " ◯◯◯◯
here

JUMBLE®

Unscramble these four Jumbles, one letter to each square, to form four ordinary words.

DYNAH

ALTNA

TEVVLE

NIPPEG

I'm a sucker for blue eyes like yours

Just punch my ticket, Buster

WHAT THE SMOOTH-TALKING CONDUC-TOR RAN INTO.

Now arrange the circled letters to form the surprise answer, as suggested by the above cartoon.

Print answer here ◯◯◯ ◯◯◯ OF THE "◯◯◯◯"

JUMBLE®

Unscramble these four Jumbles, one letter to each square, to form four ordinary words.

VABOE

NOWRC

GOFTER

DEBALF

That's it ---300!

WHEN HE ROLLED
A PERFECT GAME
HIS OPPONENT
WAS ----

Now arrange the circled letters to form the surprise answer, as suggested by the above cartoon.

Print
answer
here

" ◯◯◯◯◯◯ " ◯◯◯◯

JUMBLE®

Unscramble these four Jumbles, one letter to each square, to form four ordinary words.

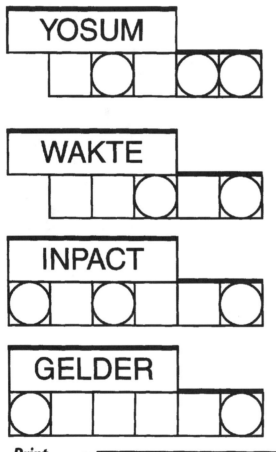

YOSUM

WAKTE

INPACT

GELDER

I can double your money

NO!!

AN UNSOLICITED CALL FROM A BROKER CAN RESULT IN THIS.

Now arrange the circled letters to form the surprise answer, as suggested by the above cartoon.

Print answer here A " ◯◯◯◯◯ " ◯◯◯◯◯

JUMBLE®

Unscramble these four Jumbles, one letter to
each square, to form four ordinary words.

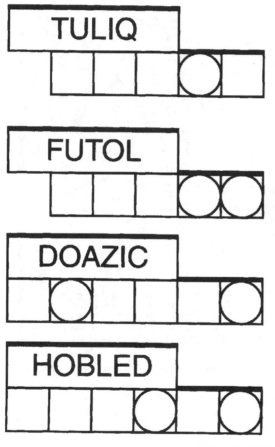

TULIQ

FUTOL

DOAZIC

HOBLED

Wha'
happened?

WHEN THE ICICLE
FELL ON HIS
HEAD HE WAS ----

Now arrange the circled letters to form the
surprise answer, as suggested by the above
cartoon.

Print answer here ◯◯◯ " ◯◯◯◯ "

JUMBLE®

Unscramble these four Jumbles, one letter to each square, to form four ordinary words.

GNUST

CRANF

NAKTIE

ZOLENZ

WHAT THE BOSS' SON USED TO GET HIS WAY.

Now arrange the circled letters to form the surprise answer, as suggested by the above cartoon.

Print answer here " ◯◯◯◯◯◯◯◯◯◯ "

JUMBLE®

Unscramble these four Jumbles, one letter to each square, to form four ordinary words.

NIFSI

NOOZE

KANTLE

RAFAIN

They were $35 last year

OUR LOW PRICE $50

THIS WILL CAUSE TIRES TO GO UP.

Now arrange the circled letters to form the surprise answer, as suggested by the above cartoon.

Print answer here

JUMBLE®

Unscramble these four Jumbles, one letter to each square, to form four ordinary words.

ARGIN

TELUF

DESEEC

GARUJA

I'll bet $1000

Too rich for me

WHAT THE POKER PLAYERS CON-SIDERED HIS BET.

Now arrange the circled letters to form the surprise answer, as suggested by the above cartoon.

Print answer here   A "◯◯◯◯◯" ◯◯◯◯◯◯◯

JUMBLE®

Unscramble these four Jumbles, one letter to each square, to form four ordinary words.

PHULS

STACE

SHAUTI

ANQUIT

They're funny

THE VISITING CLOWNS TURNED THE CHILDREN'S WARD INTO THIS.

Now arrange the circled letters to form the surprise answer, as suggested by the above cartoon.

Print answer here **A** " ◯◯ - ◯◯◯◯◯◯ "

JUMBLE®

Unscramble these four Jumbles, one letter to
each square, to form four ordinary words.

TAABE

SONIE

BUTSOE

FIVERD

That fish looks good

FOUND IN A
BUFFET-STYLE
RESTAURANT.

Now arrange the circled letters to form the
surprise answer, as suggested by the above
cartoon.

Print answer here " ◯◯◯ " ◯◯◯◯

JUMBLE®

Unscramble these four Jumbles, one letter to each square, to form four ordinary words.

CLICO

GRAWE

BRENAT

MOABEA

She's with me

That's my girl

THE ANGRY DANCERS TURNED THE DANCE HALL INTO THIS.

Now arrange the circled letters to form the surprise answer, as suggested by the above cartoon.

Print answer here A ⬚⬚⬚⬚⬚ ⬚⬚⬚⬚

JUMBLE®

Unscramble these four Jumbles, one letter to each square, to form four ordinary words.

ANCKK

LUCCK

DEMANT

CAYGLE

It's making me ill

WHAT IT FELT LIKE WHEN SHE PLAYED HER MELODY.

Now arrange the circled letters to form the surprise answer, as suggested by the above cartoon.

Print answer here **A** ⬡⬡⬡⬡⬡⬡

JUMBLE®

Unscramble these four Jumbles, one letter to each square, to form four ordinary words.

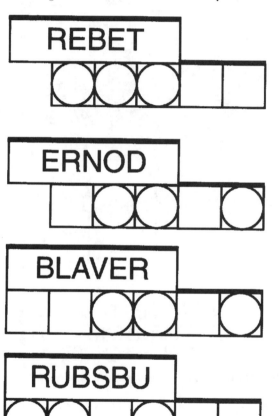

REBET

ERNOD

BLAVER

RUBSBU

Down with everybody!

ANOTHER NAME FOR A DEMOLI-TION EXPERT.

Now arrange the circled letters to form the surprise answer, as suggested by the above cartoon.

Print answer here A

JUMBLE®

Unscramble these four Jumbles, one letter to each square, to form four ordinary words.

JEDDA

DOLOF

TENCED

WULTOA

He works hard

WHAT HE DID AT THE COMPUTER STORE.

Now arrange the circled letters to form the surprise answer, as suggested by the above cartoon.

Print answer here " ☐☐☐☐ ☐☐☐☐☐☐ "

JUMBLE®

Unscramble these four Jumbles, one letter to each square, to form four ordinary words.

KWISH

CARTT

INLOPP

MULASY

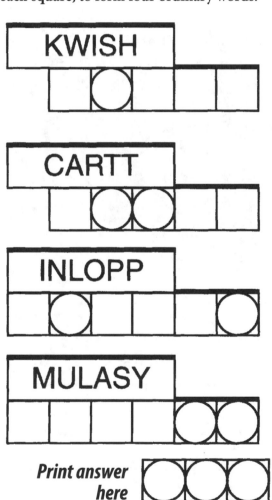

BONG BONG

He's the best

THE OLD-TIME CLOCK-MAKER WAS KNOWN AS THIS.

Now arrange the circled letters to form the surprise answer, as suggested by the above cartoon.

Print answer here ⬡⬡⬡ **OF THE** " ⬡⬡⬡⬡ "

JUMBLE®

Unscramble these four Jumbles, one letter to
each square, to form four ordinary words.

TOBOY

HAMER

DESAUB

THORCC

That's
deep

WHERE THE
EXECUTIVES MET
TO LISTEN TO
POETRY.

Now arrange the circled letters to form the
surprise answer, as suggested by the above
cartoon.

Print answer here **IN THE**

JUMBLE®

Unscramble these four Jumbles, one letter to
each square, to form four ordinary words.

MAWPS

CUSTO

USEBUD

COTESK

Here's a dollar
for ice cream

YOU MIGHT SAY
HE DID THIS
WHEN HE
STROLLED
BY THE MOOSE.

Now arrange the circled letters to form the
surprise answer, as suggested by the above
cartoon.

*Print
answer
here* ◯◯◯◯◯◯ THE ◯◯◯◯

JUMBLE®

Unscramble these four Jumbles, one letter to
each square, to form four ordinary words.

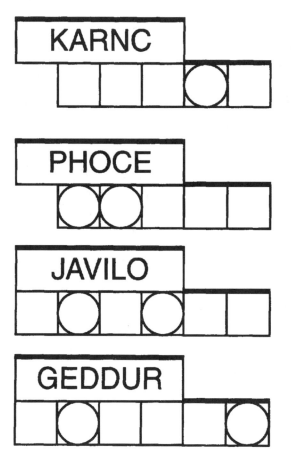

KARNC

PHOCE

JAVILO

GEDDUR

Hi, Scorpio here.
What's your sign?

WHAT SHE CON-
SIDERED HIS
ATTEMPT AT
CONVERSATION.

Now arrange the circled letters to form the
surprise answer, as suggested by the above
cartoon.

Print answer here **AN** " "

JUMBLE®

Unscramble these four Jumbles, one letter to
each square, to form four ordinary words.

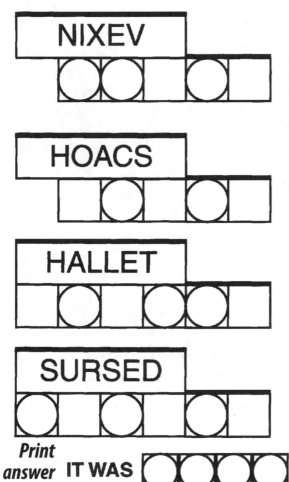

NIXEV

HOACS

HALLET

SURSED

GLUB GLUB GLUB

WHY HE NEVER
BECAME A GOOD
DIVER.

Now arrange the circled letters to form the
surprise answer, as suggested by the above
cartoon.

Print
answer
here

IT WAS

JUMBLE®

Unscramble these four Jumbles, one letter to
each square, to form four ordinary words.

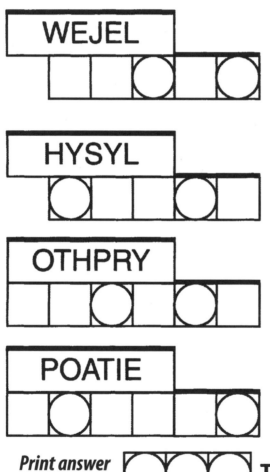

WEJEL

HYSYL

OTHPRY

POATIE

Aa Bb Cc Dd Ee Ff Gg Hh

A C-U-R-S-E
on you

WHAT THE YOUNG
WITCH LEARNED
AT SCHOOL.

Now arrange the circled letters to form the
surprise answer, as suggested by the above
cartoon.

**Print answer
here** ◯◯◯ **TO** " ◯◯◯◯◯ "

JUMBLE®

Unscramble these four Jumbles, one letter to
each square, to form four ordinary words.

PUGOR

KINDE

INLOIV

GIXNIF

Sorry, Smithers, but we're
cutting staff

WHERE THE COM-
PANY DOWNSIZING
PUT THE
MANAGER.

Now arrange the circled letters to form the
surprise answer, as suggested by the above
cartoon.

Print
answer ON
here THE "⬡⬡⬡⬡⬡⬡" ⬡⬡⬡⬡

123

JUMBLE®

Unscramble these four Jumbles, one letter to each square, to form four ordinary words.

CLECY

OAQUT

GICART

MACTIP

Approved, next

WHAT THE INSPEC-
TOR CONSIDERED
HER WORKING
HOURS.

Now arrange the circled letters to form the surprise answer, as suggested by the above cartoon.

Print answer here " ☐☐☐☐☐☐☐ " ☐☐☐☐

JUMBLE®

Unscramble these four Jumbles, one letter to each square, to form four ordinary words.

EGGAU

DEGIM

GLEMIT

GIZHAN

WHY DID THE HUNGRY DINER COMPLAIN ABOUT THE LONG WAIT?

Now arrange the circled letters to form the surprise answer, as suggested by the above cartoon.

Print answer here IT WAS ⬡⬡⬡⬡⬡⬡ ⬡⬡⬡

JUMBLE®

Unscramble these four Jumbles, one letter to
each square, to form four ordinary words.

KLABY

HECEL

ANTUSE

PAMEND

Make sure you add
flour as needed

What did I
do wrong?

WHAT AN
INSTRUCTOR
DOES AT
BAKING SCHOOL.

Now arrange the circled letters to form the
surprise answer, as suggested by the above
cartoon.

Print
answer
here

THE

JUMBLE®

Unscramble these four Jumbles, one letter to each square, to form four ordinary words.

OMENG

YINSH

BROMEY

CIPCIN

He never stops

Always looking for a bargain

THE TIGHTWAD IN-VESTOR WATCHED THIS ON-LINE.

Now arrange the circled letters to form the surprise answer, as suggested by the above cartoon.

Print answer here

JUMBLE

Unscramble these four Jumbles, one letter to each square, to form four ordinary words.

HAFFC

DANGL

INCLOU

GARNAL

Yes, tell me about your unwanted offer. Dinner can wait

WHAT THE COMEDIAN WAS KNOWN AS FOR HIS TELEPHONE ROUTINE.

Now arrange the circled letters to form the surprise answer, as suggested by the above cartoon.

Print answer here A ☐☐☐☐☐☐☐☐ "☐☐☐☐"

JUMBLE®

Unscramble these four Jumbles, one letter to
each square, to form four ordinary words.

NOLFE

DACKE

THIRDE

SEECIX

Gotta get into a business
that pays real money

WHAT HE
CONSIDERED
THE TINY PROFITS
FROM HIS EGG
FARM.

Now arrange the circled letters to form the
surprise answer, as suggested by the above
cartoon.

Print
answer
here

JUMBLE®

Unscramble these four Jumbles, one letter to each square, to form four ordinary words.

GOMAD

LARRU

ASCUBA

CRUSHO

The turnoff must be carefully graded

He knows everything

WHAT THE EXPERT ON HIGHWAYS WAS CONSIDERED BY HIS PEERS.

Now arrange the circled letters to form the surprise answer, as suggested by the above cartoon.

Print answer here A " ⬡⬡⬡⬡⬡ " ⬡⬡⬡⬡⬡⬡⬡

JUMBLE®

Unscramble these four Jumbles, one letter to each square, to form four ordinary words.

REXTE

LAANC

DOAFER

NAHRGE

THIS HAPPENED TO THE RUNNER WHO FELL IN LOVE.

Now arrange the circled letters to form the surprise answer, as suggested by the above cartoon.

Print answer here   HIS

JUMBLE®

Unscramble these four Jumbles, one letter to each square, to form four ordinary words.

KICCH

THANC

BELMAG

GLOONB

There goes Louie

WHAT THE RETIRED BARBER ENDED UP DOING.

Now arrange the circled letters to form the surprise answer, as suggested by the above cartoon.

Print answer here

JUMBLE®

Unscramble these four Jumbles, one letter to
each square, to form four ordinary words.

THEFY

ANIFT

DORICH

TEAGEN

I wonder what it's
supposed to be

IMPORTANT TO
GET
WHEN WORKING IN
AN ART GALLERY.

Now arrange the circled letters to form the
surprise answer, as suggested by the above
cartoon.

Print answer here THE ⬡⬡⬡⬡ ⬡⬡ ⬡⬡

JUMBLE®

Unscramble these four Jumbles, one letter to each square, to form four ordinary words.

SUDOE

FLATA

EXNOST

SHRAID

Oh, no --- I'll have to throw it away!

WHAT MOM ENDED UP WITH WHEN TOO MUCH VINE-GAR WAS POURED.

Now arrange the circled letters to form the surprise answer, as suggested by the above cartoon.

Print answer here " ◯◯◯◯◯◯ " ◯◯◯◯◯

JUMBLE®

Unscramble these four Jumbles, one letter to each square, to form four ordinary words.

STUJO

HEGIT

SILFOS

ROTTAH

He's getting Ms. LaFemme to pose

I plan to be the best

THE AMBITIOUS PHOTOGRAPHER DECIDED TO ----

Now arrange the circled letters to form the surprise answer, as suggested by the above cartoon.

Print answer here

FOR THE

JUMBLE®

Unscramble these four Jumbles, one letter to
each square, to form four ordinary words.

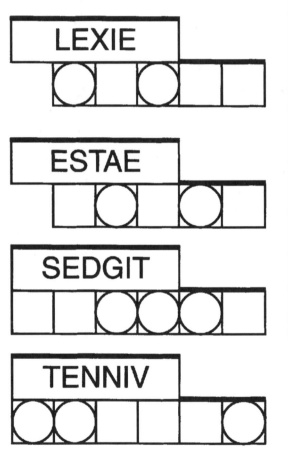

LEXIE

ESTAE

SEDGIT

TENNIV

Looks promising, let's
do some research

BUILDING
FOR SALE

INVESTING IN
PROPERTY
INVOLVES THIS.

Now arrange the circled letters to form the
surprise answer, as suggested by the above
cartoon.

*Print answer
here*

JUMBLE®

Unscramble these four Jumbles, one letter to
each square, to form four ordinary words.

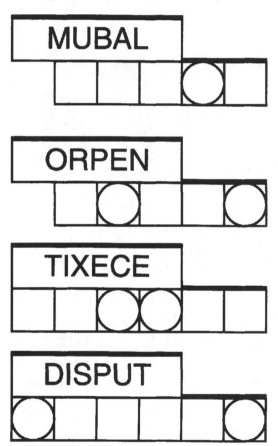

MUBAL

ORPEN

TIXECE

DISPUT

ARCADE

FUN HOUSE

TATTOOS

So much to do

WHAT THE
SAILORS
DID ON SHORE
LEAVE.

Now arrange the circled letters to form the
surprise answer, as suggested by the above
cartoon.

Print answer here

137

JUMBLE®

Unscramble these four Jumbles, one letter to each square, to form four ordinary words.

COTIN

RABIR

TINISS

GIFFEY

Beautiful

... and a great fullback

WHERE THE VIOLIN-PLAYING FOOTBALL PLAYER ENDED UP.

Now arrange the circled letters to form the surprise answer, as suggested by the above cartoon.

Print answer here **THE**

JUMBLE®

Unscramble these four Jumbles, one letter to each square, to form four ordinary words.

CIKHT

MOIFT

ETOGEA

OOTARR

You're grounded this weekend

WHAT JUNIOR FACED WHEN HE FLUNKED THE FRACTIONS TEST.

Now arrange the circled letters to form the surprise answer, as suggested by the above cartoon.

Print answer here **THE** " ◯◯◯◯◯◯ - ◯◯◯◯ "

JUMBLE

Unscramble these four Jumbles, one letter to
each square, to form four ordinary words.

GLIBE

LIENN

BRUZZE

ZEEWEH

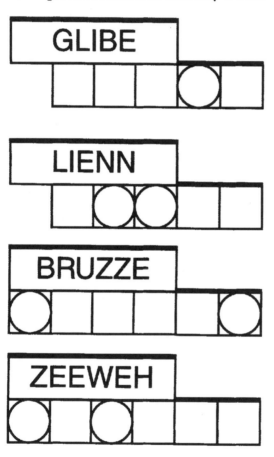

It's your turn to
make the coffee

No,
yours

WHY THE MANAGER
WASN'T SUR-
PRISED WHEN THE
WAITRESSES
ARGUED.

Now arrange the circled letters to form the
surprise answer, as suggested by the above
cartoon.

Print answer here   **IT WAS**

JUMBLE®

Unscramble these four Jumbles, one letter to each square, to form four ordinary words.

ENPOY

RAFOL

PHONTY

VEEVOL

It's not you, it's me

WHEN A RELATION-
SHIP SOURS
THEY'RE
EASY TO SEE.

Now arrange the circled letters to form the surprise answer, as suggested by the above cartoon.

Print answer here

JUMBLE®

Unscramble these four Jumbles, one letter to
each square, to form four ordinary words.

GEDEW

AGELL

BABFLY

VAUDLE

All she does is cry

WHAT THE BROTH-
ERS CALLED THEIR
NEWBORN SISTER.

Now arrange the circled letters to form the
surprise answer, as suggested by the above
cartoon.

*Print
answer
here*   THE ◯◯◯◯◯◯ OF THE " ◯◯◯◯ "

JUMBLE®

Unscramble these four Jumbles, one letter to
each square, to form four ordinary words.

GATEA

KOHCE

ACTUFE

NAIGAN

So appealing

WHAT THE
ARTIST'S
PORTRAYAL OF
THE SHOW DOG
WAS CONSIDERED.

Now arrange the circled letters to form the
surprise answer, as suggested by the above
cartoon.

Print answer here

JUMBLE®

Unscramble these four Jumbles, one letter to
each square, to form four ordinary words.

SONEO

DEALL

HERZIT

VAQUER

GETTING THE
MOST CARDS ON
VALENTINE'S DAY
MADE HER THIS.

Now arrange the circled letters to form the
surprise answer, as suggested by the above
cartoon.

*Print
answer
here* THE ⬡⬡⬡⬡⬡ OF ⬡⬡⬡⬡⬡⬡

JUMBLE®

Unscramble these four Jumbles, one letter to
each square, to form four ordinary words.

FIDUL

SCERS

WHERDS

FONZER

You're both
losing weight

Time to take
care of
ourselves

FOR
SALE

WHAT THE OVER-
WEIGHT EMPTY
NESTERS DID.

Now arrange the circled letters to form the
surprise answer, as suggested by the above
cartoon.

Print answer here

JUMBLE®

Unscramble these four Jumbles, one letter to each square, to form four ordinary words.

NEEYM

YALLD

HOGNIM

SEATTE

Outstanding work, my boy

THE JEWELER'S TRANSACTION TURNED OUT TO BE THIS.

Now arrange the circled letters to form the surprise answer, as suggested by the above cartoon.

Print answer here A ◯◯◯ OF A ◯◯◯◯

JUMBLE®

Unscramble these four Jumbles, one letter to
each square, to form four ordinary words.

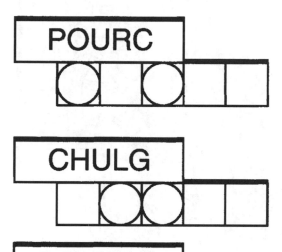

POURC

CHULG

ROGERF

ORMMEY

Back to work! Time is money

Yes, sir

Right away, sir

IMPORTANT TO
KEEP WHEN THE
BOSS GETS HOT.

Now arrange the circled letters to form the
surprise answer, as suggested by the above
cartoon.

Print answer here

JUMBLE®

Unscramble these four Jumbles, one letter to each square, to form four ordinary words.

WETET

TAPAD

VITHER

TOWPUN

She's tripled her income

WHAT IT TAKES
TO SUCCEED WITH
A HOROSCOPE
WEB SITE.

Now arrange the circled letters to form the surprise answer, as suggested by the above cartoon.

Print answer here A " ☐☐☐ " ☐☐☐☐☐☐☐

JUMBLE®

Unscramble these four Jumbles, one letter to
each square, to form four ordinary words.

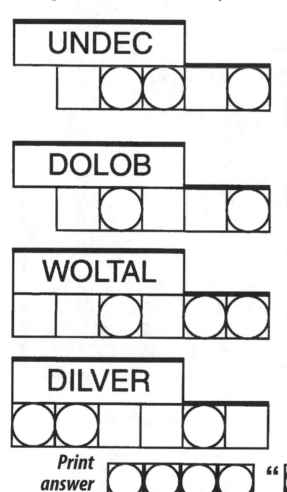

UNDEC

DOLOB

WOLTAL

DILVER

All this learning
makes me hungry

MIDNIGHT SNACKS
WHILE STUDYING
HELPED HIM
BECOME THIS.

Now arrange the circled letters to form the
surprise answer, as suggested by the above
cartoon.

Print
answer
here   ◯◯◯◯ " ◯◯◯◯◯◯◯◯ "

JUMBLE®

Unscramble these four Jumbles, one letter to
each square, to form four ordinary words.

DENEY

CELRE

TURTEG

COWLAL

That's a take

He makes it
so believable

WHAT THE DIREC-
TOR CAPTURED IN
THE MOVIE ABOUT
HOLLYWOOD.

Now arrange the circled letters to form the
surprise answer, as suggested by the above
cartoon.

**Print answer
here** THE ⭕⭕⭕⭕⭕ ⭕⭕⭕⭕⭕⭕

JUMBLE®

Unscramble these four Jumbles, one letter to
each square, to form four ordinary words.

DRYIT

FOOLI

ENGOUL

FLIPER

She's a good mother

She's our new star

WHAT THE LION-
ESS BECAME WHEN
THE CUBS WERE
BORN.

Now arrange the circled letters to form the
surprise answer, as suggested by the above
cartoon.

Print answer here " ◯◯◯◯◯ - ◯◯◯◯ "

JUMBLE®

Unscramble these four Jumbles, one letter to
each square, to form four ordinary words.

RYHUR

CAPEN

REJUIN

CATATH

No, thanks. I prefer coffee

SOME SPURN THIS
ENGLISH RITUAL
BECAUSE IT'S
NOT ---

Now arrange the circled letters to form the
surprise answer, as suggested by the above
cartoon.

Print answer here

OF

JUMBLE®

Unscramble these four Jumbles, one letter to
each square, to form four ordinary words.

NEQUE

BIRAB

CHOTLE

KITSCY

My hands
are raw

Ouch, my
back

WHAT THE FARM
HANDS TURNED
INTO AFTER
HOEING ALL
THE FIELDS.

Now arrange the circled letters to form the
surprise answer, as suggested by the above
cartoon.

Print answer here " ◯◯◯◯◯ - ◯◯◯ "

JUMBLE®

Unscramble these four Jumbles, one letter to
each square, to form four ordinary words.

VIALE

SURBT

LUCKES

PAMNEC

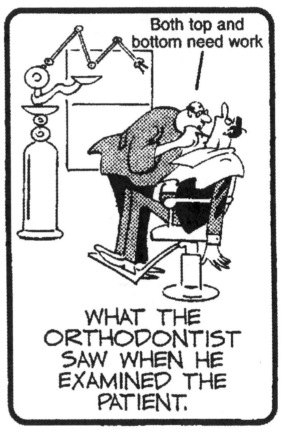

Both top and
bottom need work

WHAT THE
ORTHODONTIST
SAW WHEN HE
EXAMINED THE
PATIENT.

Now arrange the circled letters to form the
surprise answer, as suggested by the above
cartoon.

*Print
answer
here*

FOR

JUMBLE®

Unscramble these four Jumbles, one letter to each square, to form four ordinary words.

YARPT

UNREP

NUDEAS

GINTRY

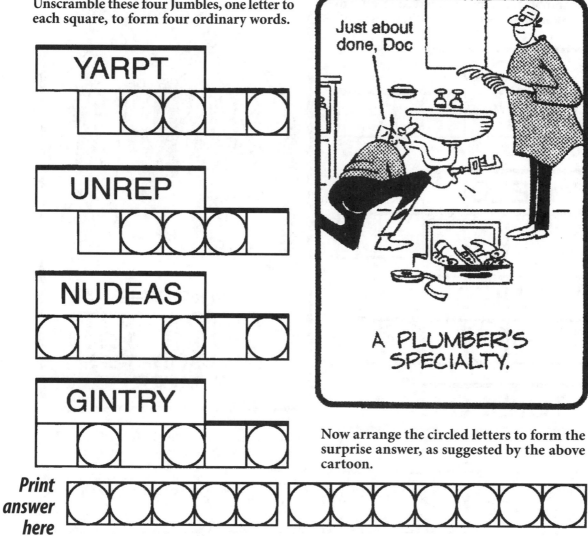

Just about done, Doc

A PLUMBER'S SPECIALTY.

Now arrange the circled letters to form the surprise answer, as suggested by the above cartoon.

Print answer here

JUMBLE®

Unscramble these four Jumbles, one letter to each square, to form four ordinary words.

GLOIC

GEEBI

RUJITS

TOLBEG

I've gained a son

WHAT THE SENATOR ENDED UP WITH WHEN HIS DAUGHTER GOT MARRIED.

Now arrange the circled letters to form the surprise answer, as suggested by the above cartoon.

Print answer here THE ⬡⬡⬡⬡⬡ OF ⬡⬡⬡⬡⬡⬡

JUMBLE®

Unscramble these four Jumbles, one letter to each square, to form four ordinary words.

BEDAK

OMBOL

GONING

HERNET

I can't wait to do this again!

What a whopper!

THIS HAPPENED ON HIS FIRST FISHING TRIP.

Now arrange the circled letters to form the surprise answer, as suggested by the above cartoon.

Print answer here **HE** ◯◯◯ ◯◯◯◯◯◯◯

JUMBLE®

Unscramble these four Jumbles, one letter to
each square, to form four ordinary words.

BISSA

ZIRPE

JELOTS

NORBEK

See? Nothing
to it

WHAT HE SAID
AFTER HE IN-
STALLED THE FAN.

Now arrange the circled letters to form the
surprise answer, as suggested by the above
cartoon.

*Print
answer
here* " ◯◯ ' ◯ A ◯◯◯◯◯◯◯ "

JUMBLE®

Unscramble these four Jumbles, one letter to
each square, to form four ordinary words.

WECIT

FLOYT

LOUTTE

HUGNOE

All clear ahead

ARCTIC SAILORS
OFTEN DO THIS.

Now arrange the circled letters to form the
surprise answer, as suggested by the above
cartoon.

Print
answer
here

THE

JUMBLE®

Unscramble these four Jumbles, one letter to
each square, to form four ordinary words.

YACED

BEDIP

INGEEN

BATERY

We'll have a fresh
salad tonight

WHAT HER VEGE-
TABLE PATCH
TURNED INTO.

Now arrange the circled letters to form the
surprise answer, as suggested by the above
cartoon.

*Print
answer
here*   A ☐◯◯◯◯◯◯ OF ◯◯◯◯◯ '

JUMBLE®

Unscramble these four Jumbles, one letter to
each square, to form four ordinary words.

NIGTY

RUGAU

STEBIC

STAFLE

This will
keep the
fleas away

MOM SPRAYED THE
NEW PUPPIES TO
AVOID THIS.

Now arrange the circled letters to form the
surprise answer, as suggested by the above
cartoon.

Print
answer
here   "⬡⬡⬡⬡⬡⬡" ⬡⬡⬡⬡

JUMBLE®

Unscramble these four Jumbles, one letter to each square, to form four ordinary words.

DRUGO

MODEN

RAYLEY

HIRTHE

Guess it's time for milking

WHAT THE COWS DID WHEN SHE RANG THE DINNER BELL.

Now arrange the circled letters to form the surprise answer, as suggested by the above cartoon.

Print answer here **THE** ⬡⬡⬡⬡ ⬡⬡⬡⬡⬡

JUMBLE®

Unscramble these six Jumbles, one letter to each square, to form six ordinary words.

VENCOL

SCUSID

RUMMRU

ENTODE

TRAFOC

SOACLE

We need pads, man

I'm not sure we have room

WHAT THE HOTEL MANAGER HAD WHEN THE ROWDY GROUP ARRIVED.

Now arrange the circled letters to form the surprise answer, as suggested by the above cartoon.

Print answer here

JUMBLE®

Unscramble these six Jumbles, one letter to each square, to form six ordinary words.

NISUFE

YATGIE

PROPHE

MYTIES

DAILIN

RADAIF

Bill gets the shop, and Bob gets the house

He promised me the house!

WHAT THE BARBER'S WILL ENDED UP DOING.

Now arrange the circled letters to form the surprise answer, as suggested by the above cartoon.

Print answer here

JUMBLE

Unscramble these six Jumbles, one letter to each square, to form six ordinary words.

POURRA

TERRAY

AIRFUN

UNCANE

LACKAJ

MELVUL

Hey, you're making more work for me

MANY DO THIS IN THE FALL.

Now arrange the circled letters to form the surprise answer, as suggested by the above cartoon.

Print answer here

 AN OLD

166

JUMBLE®

Unscramble these six Jumbles, one letter to each square, to form six ordinary words.

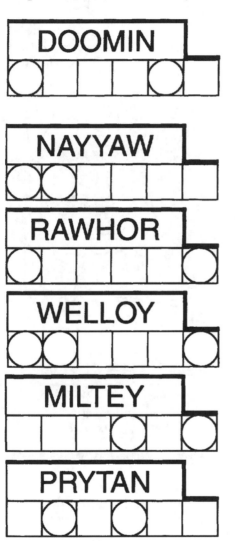

DOOMIN

NAYYAW

RAWHOR

WELLOY

MILTEY

PRYTAN

I didn't get any rest

WHAT HE FACED AFTER A SLEEP-LESS NIGHT.

Now arrange the circled letters to form the surprise answer, as suggested by the above cartoon.

Print answer here

◯◯◯ ◯◯◯◯◯ **OF A** ◯◯◯ ◯◯◯

JUMBLE

Unscramble these six Jumbles, one letter to each square, to form six ordinary words.

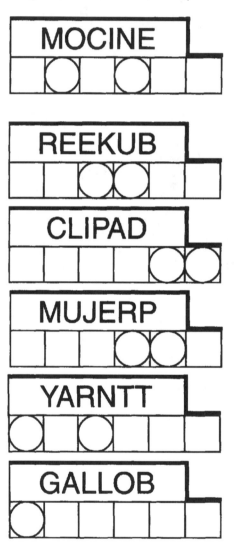

MOCINE

REEKUB

CLIPAD

MUJERP

YARNTT

GALLOB

He's funny looking

WHERE THE CLOWN ENDED UP WHEN HE LET HIS HAIR GROW.

Now arrange the circled letters to form the surprise answer, as suggested by the above cartoon.

Print answer here

 **THE**  "  "

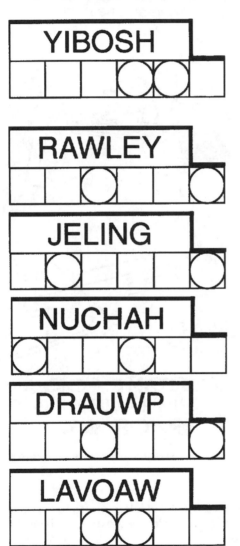

JUMBLE

Unscramble these six Jumbles, one letter to each square, to form six ordinary words.

YIBOSH

RAWLEY

JELING

NUCHAH

DRAUWP

LAVOAW

Will Santa bring them?

WHAT THE CHRISTMAS DISPLAY TURNED THE KID INTO.

Now arrange the circled letters to form the surprise answer, as suggested by the above cartoon.

Print answer here

A

169

JUMBLE®

Unscramble these six Jumbles, one letter to
each square, to form six ordinary words.

YUNCAL

REGEME

FLYTAL

BRANER

DEBBAL

DOMBEY

This will keep you
strong and healthy

IMPORTANT FOR A
HIGH-WIRE
PERFORMER.

Now arrange the circled letters to form the
surprise answer, as suggested by the above
cartoon.

Print answer here

A " _____ " ____

JUMBLE®

Unscramble these six Jumbles, one letter to each square, to form six ordinary words.

BLUHME

BRATIB

TEABED

DIPEEM

BINNOR

YECTIN

We needed it

THE VILLAGERS SAID THE NEW CLOCK TOWER WAS ----

Now arrange the circled letters to form the surprise answer, as suggested by the above cartoon.

Print answer here

A

JUMBLE

Unscramble these six Jumbles, one letter to each square, to form six ordinary words.

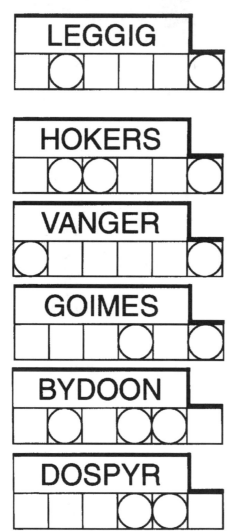

LEGGIG

HOKERS

VANGER

GOIMES

BYDOON

DOSPYR

Play it again, Sam

He's terrific

EASILY MADE BY A TOP-NOTCH MIMIC.

Now arrange the circled letters to form the surprise answer, as suggested by the above cartoon.

Print answer here

A

JUMBLE®

Unscramble these six Jumbles, one letter to each square, to form six ordinary words.

LOWLAF

ZARDAH

YABSUW

LAMAMM

CALARI

COOTLE

... and the meat was tough

PAYING FOR A FANCY MEAL CAN BECOME THIS.

Now arrange the circled letters to form the surprise answer, as suggested by the above cartoon.

Print answer here

⬡⬡⬡⬡ TO ⬡⬡⬡⬡⬡⬡⬡

JUMBLE®

Unscramble these six Jumbles, one letter to each square, to form six ordinary words.

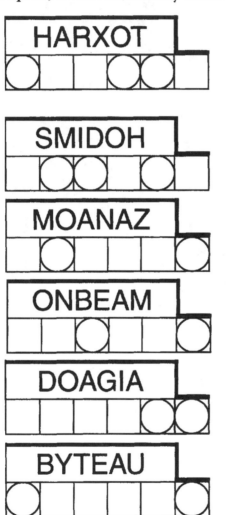

HARXOT

SMIDOH

MOANAZ

ONBEAM

DOAGIA

BYTEAU

In a few years we'll double our money

TELLER

WHAT THE COUPLE ENJOYED AFTER THE WEDDING.

Now arrange the circled letters to form the surprise answer, as suggested by the above cartoon.

Print answer here

THE ⬡⬡⬡⬡⬡ OF ⬡⬡⬡⬡⬡⬡⬡⬡⬡

JUMBLE®

Unscramble these six Jumbles, one letter to each square, to form six ordinary words.

PLAACA

DRIVEA

HARTER

SHUHRT

SHABIN

GURFEE

Oh, I love it

CUTTING HER TRESSES GAVE HER THIS.

Now arrange the circled letters to form the surprise answer, as suggested by the above cartoon.

Print answer here

" ⬡⬡⬡⬡⬡ " ⬡⬡⬡⬡⬡⬡⬡⬡⬡

JUMBLE®

Unscramble these six Jumbles, one letter to each square, to form six ordinary words.

REVOUD

HEWPEN

COSTAM

DUGIED

JURNIY

EURUFT

What are the issues in next week's election?

I know

THE ELECTRICIAN'S FAVORITE SUBJECT IN NIGHT SCHOOL.

Now arrange the circled letters to form the surprise answer, as suggested by the above cartoon.

Print answer here

" ⬡⬡⬡⬡⬡⬡⬡ " ⬡⬡⬡⬡⬡⬡

JUMBLE®

Unscramble these six Jumbles, one letter to each square, to form six ordinary words.

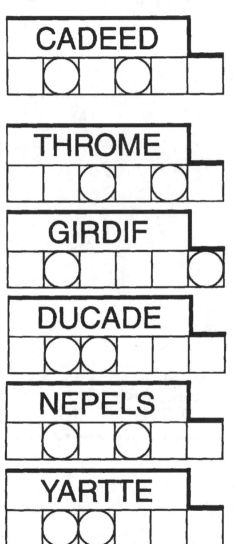

CADEED

THROME

GIRDIF

DUCADE

NEPELS

YARTTE

Haven't seen a buck in two days

They must have gone south

THIS ALWAYS SADDENS HUNTERS.

Now arrange the circled letters to form the surprise answer, as suggested by the above cartoon.

Print answer here

THE ⬡⬡⬡⬡⬡ ⬡⬡⬡⬡⬡⬡⬡⬡⬡

JUMBLE®

Unscramble these six Jumbles, one letter to
each square, to form six ordinary words.

GAAMED

GLARBE

VAINED

CRAIPY

GUBBED

NELKEN

See? They're ready to
flower

Nice job. You're
going places

A JOB AT A
NURSERY CAN
LEAD TO THIS.

Now arrange the circled letters to form the
surprise answer, as suggested by the above
cartoon.

Print answer here

A " ◯◯◯◯◯◯◯ " ◯◯◯◯◯◯◯

JUMBLE®

Unscramble these six Jumbles, one letter to each square, to form six ordinary words.

GROJAN

CHANIG

YONNAC

HOPOUK

AECIPE

HOCORB

Do we dare wake him?

He likes his 40 winks during lunch hour

THE CLERKS WERE RELUCTANT TO DO THIS WHEN THE JUDGE NAPPED IN THE PARK.

Now arrange the circled letters to form the surprise answer, as suggested by the above cartoon.

Print answer here

⬡⬡⬡⬡⬡⬡⬡⬡ THE ⬡⬡⬡⬡⬡

JUMBLE®

Unscramble these six Jumbles, one letter to each square, to form six ordinary words.

CRANEL

MICOPY

KLINTE

MEAPER

JYLFOU

TARROM

Another sale!

He always makes his quota

THE SALESMAN SOLD INSURANCE BECAUSE IT WAS A ---

Now arrange the circled letters to form the surprise answer, as suggested by the above cartoon.

Print answer here

" "

JUMBLE®

Unscramble these six Jumbles, one letter to each square, to form six ordinary words.

YEMDOC

DOLFYN

SNULES

FILMAY

FLUGEN

RISDAM

No TV for a week

WHAT JUNIOR DID WHEN HE WAS CAUGHT NOT DO-ING HIS HOME-WORK.

Now arrange the circled letters to form the surprise answer, as suggested by the above cartoon.

Print answer here

HIS

JUMBLE

Unscramble these six Jumbles, one letter to each square, to form six ordinary words.

LOOSCH

HENUCQ

FENTAS

TONKYT

HISVAL

UNIMME

Let me show you an easier way

WHY THE SERGEANT HELPED THE RE-CRUIT POLISH HIS BOOTS.

Now arrange the circled letters to form the surprise answer, as suggested by the above cartoon.

Print answer here

HE ⬡⬡⬡⬡⬡ A ⬡⬡⬡⬡⬡⬡ TO ⬡⬡⬡

JUMBLE®

Unscramble these six Jumbles, one letter to each square, to form six ordinary words.

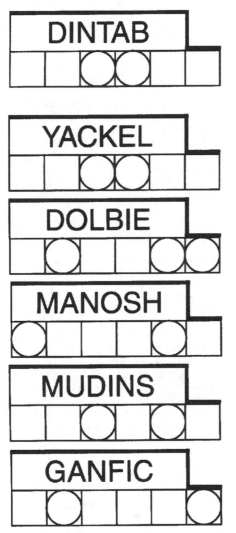

DINTAB

YACKEL

DOLBIE

MANOSH

MUDINS

GANFIC

May I offer you anything?

Yeah, more hearts

WHAT THE BRIDGE PLAYERS WANTED ON THE CRUISE.

Now arrange the circled letters to form the surprise answer, as suggested by the above cartoon.

Print answer here

"   "

ANSWERS

1. **Jumbles:** KITTY LINEN CAMPER SALOON
   Answer: What the ancient Romans could do easily that most moderns have difficulty doing—SPEAK LATIN

2. **Jumbles:** PATIO SCOUR ARCTIC IMPACT
   Answer: "Haven't you ever seen this?"—"A COMIC STRIP"

3. **Jumbles:** ITCHY FLAKE DEFILE WALRUS
   Answer: After another woman had "turned" his head, he obviously couldn't do this anymore—FACE HIS WIFE

4. **Jumbles:** LIVEN FLUID INNING DEFAME
   Answer: The dentist grew fat because almost everything he touched was this—FILLING

5. **Jumbles:** DUNCE GAUDY INVERT BODILY
   Answer: What did the bored cow say when she got up in the morning?—"JUST AN UDDER DAY"

6. **Jumbles:** GLEAM TYING PANTRY SCHEME
   Answer: How does a baby chick fit into its shell?—"EGGSACTLY"

7. **Jumbles:** HYENA SPURN BUSILY POMADE
   Answer: What do you get when you cross a cactus with a porcupine?—SORE HANDS

8. **Jumbles:** AGENT BALKY INLAND BESIDE
   Answer: What brings flowers?—THE "STALK"

9. **Jumbles:** FISHY DITTO TINKLE BELFRY
   Answer: Kids' clothes will stay clean much longer if you keep them this—OFF KIDS

10. **Jumbles:** ALIVE CIVIL EITHER BALSAM
    Answer: What do liars do after they die?—LIE STILL

11. **Jumbles:** PANDA BILGE REFUGE GOSPEL
    Answer: The little witch had to stand in the corner because she was this—A BAD "SPELLER"

12. **Jumbles:** YOUTH BEIGE HANGER CONVOY
    Answer: What the doctor said about the condition of the guy who had swallowed a half-dollar—NO CHANGE YET

13. **Jumbles:** TABOO GAVEL BOUNTY DAMAGE
    Answer: The farmer became angry when someone managed to do this—GET HIS GOAT

14. **Jumbles:** AXIOM IMPEL DIVERT BYWORD
    Answer: Mom and Dad were kept awake all night while junior was having this—A "WAIL" OF A TIME

15. **Jumbles:** SWOON GRIMY ENTIRE MANAGE
    Answer: Could be instrumental in a marriage—THE ORGANIST

16. **Jumbles:** LIMBO CRUSH DETACH BAKING
    Answer: Where those old-time warriors went on their evenings off—TO A "KNIGHT CLUB"

17. **Jumbles:** SILKY PEONY MENACE SMUDGE
    Answer: What should a sword swallower eat when he's on a diet?—PINS & NEEDLES

18. **Jumbles:** STOKE ADULT BUCKLE EXCISE
    Answer: What happened to the man who sued the porter?—HE LOST HIS CASE

19. **Jumbles:** GAUZE WHISK NOUGAT TAUGHT
    Answer: What do you call it when pigs do their laundry?—HOGWASH

20. **Jumbles:** ANKLE EMPTY BEHAVE DEAFEN
    Answer: The patients didn't like that nurse because she was always trying to do this—NEEDLE THEM

21. **Jumbles:** EXULT MOURN GUILTY PALACE
    Answer: What tequila is—THE "GULP" OF MEXICO

22. **Jumbles:** USURP OFTEN POCKET NOODLE
    Answer: If you want to buy a good wig, you sure have this—TOUPEE FOR IT

23. **Jumbles:** ABOUT INKED BLOODY INHALE
    Answer: "What's wrong with eating this little ol' apple?"—"O.K., I'LL BITE"

24. **Jumbles:** AGATE PRONE CELERY HAPPEN
    Answer: Why next year is a good year for kangaroos—IT'S "LEAP" YEAR

25. **Jumbles:** WIPED NATAL PLENTY ARTERY
    Answer: What the big game was when they put their star mummy in as pinch hitter—ALL WRAPPED UP

26. **Jumbles:** EJECT DANDY MUFFLE ENZYME
    Answer: What the knitters did when she made the sleeve too long—NEEDLED HER

27. **Jumbles:** ENTRY APPLY PUSHER EROTIC
    Answer: That gardener was known for remarks like this—"EARTHY" ONES

28. **Jumbles:** HAVOC KETCH GIGOLO UTMOST
    Answer: What the electrician-turned-pickpocket had—A "LIGHT" TOUCH

29. **Jumbles:** HITCH IMBUE SCROLL LAGOON
    Answer: Rarely performed by a doctor—A HOUSE CALL

30. **Jumbles:** BORAX GLADE JUNIOR JOCUND
    Answer: She said this when hubby mended his sock—"DARN" GOOD JOB

31. **Jumbles:** FAULT CLOAK PETITE BUMPER
    Answer: What they called that comical surgeon—A REAL CUTUP

32. **Jumbles:** HUSKY MINUS INWARD BEAGLE
    Answer: She wanted to meet the sprinter because he was—DASHING

33. **Jumbles:** ELUDE LEAVE ENDURE FLORID
    Answer: What the dentist did for his patient—"FILLED" A NEED

34. **Jumbles:** SKULK LINER FRUGAL LARYNX
    Answer: The geometry teacher was tough to fool because she knew—ALL THE ANGLES

35. **Jumbles:** EVOKE SYNOD BECKON BECOME
    Answer: What the shady restaurant owner did for the tax collector—COOKED THE BOOKS

36. **Jumbles:** VIGIL BRAWL COUPON CHEERY
    Answer: The kids liked bananas because they were—"A-PEELING"

37. **Jumbles:** RAVEN ARRAY HOMAGE SHERRY
    Answer: What daily target practice made him feel like—HOME ON THE RANGE

38. **Jumbles:** PLUME BYLAW CHOSEN HECTIC
    Answer: A doctor and his dog can keep doing this—HEAL AND HEEL

39. **Jumbles:** SPURN HELLO STIGMA FILLET
    Answer: What the unhappy transmission mechanic decided to do—SHIFT GEARS

40. **Jumbles:** CRAZE BOWER THWART DOOMED
    Answer: The street artist liked to do this—"DRAW" A CROWD

41. **Jumbles:** EMBER ACRID FRACAS ARMADA
    Answer: What the clown did at the clock factory—MADE FACES

42. **Jumbles:** WOMEN POWER BLOUSE DROWSY
    Answer: A fireman's job has this—ITS UPS AND DOWNS

43. **Jumbles:** WHEAT SCOUR SATIRE GHETTO
    Answer: What the kids said the author of spooky stories was—A GHOST WRITER

44. **Jumbles:** VALVE WINCE LIZARD BELLOW
    Answer: When a steak is cooked to perfection it becomes this—WELL DONE

45. **Jumbles:** SMOKY LATCH APATHY UNLIKE
    Answer: It takes this to feather a chicken—LOTS OF PLUCK

46. **Jumbles:** TRILL SHEAF ELIXIR PREFER
    Answer: What the investor wanted for a rainy day—A SHELTER

47. **Jumbles:** CUBIC RAPID CARNAL BENUMB
    Answer: Why he took the dirty job—TO CLEAN UP

184

48. **Jumbles:** BLAZE GLEAM MUSCLE SPORTY
Answer: What the zoo needed to pay for its new animals—A "BEASTLY" SUM

49. **Jumbles:** WHILE EAGLE MARLIN WEAKEN
Answer: Introduced by the dry cleaner to increase business—A NEW WRINKLE

50. **Jumbles:** RANCH MUSIC TALKER GROTTO
Answer: The conductor was promoted because he was—ON THE RIGHT "TRACK"

51. **Jumbles:** PERKY BUXOM VOLUME DEFAME
Answer: What the unhappy roommate forced the chess whiz to do—MAKE A MOVE

52. **Jumbles:** MAGIC ONION BIGAMY DOUBLE
Answer: What the computer operator ended up doing on her day off—GOING ON LINE

53. **Jumbles:** DOILY SKUNK FLIMSY GUITAR
Answer: How the dump left the neighbors—FUMING

54. **Jumbles:** PLAID FORTY DUPLEX BLUISH
Answer: What the séance became—SPIRITED

55. **Jumbles:** MOURN ANISE SOOTHE EMPLOY
Answer: This will make a hypochondriac sick—NO SYMPTOMS

56. **Jumbles:** BATHE UNITY EYELET EMPIRE
Answer: What the students called the mail carrier and the athlete—LETTER MEN

57. **Jumbles:** TUNED PAPER WHENCE BUCKLE
Answer: What the janitor did during his lunch break—CLEANED UP

58. **Jumbles:** TABOO GRIMY HANDLE EXHALE
Answer: Important to do after a skiing accident—HANG IN THERE

59. **Jumbles:** AIDED INLET FEWEST VIABLE
Answer: What Dad's old school neckwear became—THE TIE THAT BINDS

60. **Jumbles:** TACKY FAITH CENSUS FACIAL
Answer: A successful race car driver does this—THINKS "FAST"

61. **Jumbles:** VAGUE MUSTY SQUALL FLORAL
Answer: The security deposit on the apartment amounted to this—A "FLAT" SUM

62. **Jumbles:** LLAMA BLESS BEHELD NUTRIA
Answer: What the company improved with its new web site—"NET" SALES

63. **Jumbles:** PROBE DOWDY INVEST BALLET
Answer: Why they listened to his poetry—HE WAS WELL "VERSED"

64. **Jumbles:** POISE MIRTH PALLID CUDGEL
Answer: What the divorce judge gave his son—CHILD SUPPORT

65. **Jumbles:** YOKEL GRIPE HOURLY COOPER
Answer: Easy to turn into at a vacation lodge—A "ROCK" GROUP

66. **Jumbles:** AWARD DELVE IMPAIR GATHER
Answer: What the jeweler considered his hard-working clerk—A REAL GEM

67. **Jumbles:** BEGUN GUISE NATURE CACTUS
Answer: An uptight grammarian is always this—IN "TENSE"

68. **Jumbles:** DROOP SNARL PONDER MALADY
Answer: What the would-be diva turned laundry day into—A SOAP OPERA

69. **Jumbles:** CEASE WEIGH WHALER DETACH
Answer: Why she disliked the nasty shoe salesman—HE WAS A HEEL

70. **Jumbles:** HOIST FINAL BELFRY COMPEL
Answer: What the merchant realized when the negligees went on sale—A "FLIMSY" PROFIT

71. **Jumbles:** HOBBY BRIBE RECTOR MISHAP
Answer: He raced for the train and ended up short of this—HIS BREATH

72. **Jumbles:** BARON HABIT CAUGHT SOIREE
Answer: Why he never worried about renting the beach house—IT WAS A SHORE THING

73. **Jumbles:** OLDER LEAKY PLAQUE DAWNED
Answer: Before the concert the pianist was—ALL KEYED UP

74. **Jumbles:** ICING CHAFE HARBOR FALTER
Answer: Did she lose weight on the ice cream diet?—FAT CHANCE

75. **Jumbles:** ODDLY DRAMA INLAND BROGUE
Answer: What the bill collector got when the debt was finally paid—A "DUN" DEAL

76. **Jumbles:** JOKER LOONY CARPET CALMLY
Answer: What Mom wanted the kids to do when the house was a mess—COME CLEAN

77. **Jumbles:** FUROR AXIOM NIPPLE FEMALE
Answer: Layoff rumors can set this off—A "FIRE" ALARM

78. **Jumbles:** GRIME MADLY POTTER DISOWN
Answer: What the server became when the cook fell behind—A WAITER

79. **Jumbles:** EXULT MOUSE BRANCH WIDEST
Answer: She got candy because he was—SWEET ON HER

80. **Jumbles:** HAZEL DADDY HEREBY LIMBER
Answer: The batting star got the big contract by playing—"HARDBALL"

81. **Jumbles:** DUMPY OWING MOTION GOSPEL
Answer: Where the injured lumberjack ended up after treatment—OUT OF THE WOODS

82. **Jumbles:** LEAFY QUEUE APPALL CAVORT
Answer: What the stockbroker increased with a smile—HIS FACE VALUE

83. **Jumbles:** WHINE AGONY APPEAR STYLUS
Answer: Why the phone operator dreaded the birthday bash—PARTY "LINES"

84. **Jumbles:** AROMA CROAK HOOKED WHITEN
Answer: What the teacher did after school—HOME WORK

85. **Jumbles:** GUILT BRAIN WIZARD BRANDY
Answer: The huge mural was—A BIG "DRAW"

86. **Jumbles:** HEDGE LIGHT TWINGE WISELY
Answer: What a lot of fouls can do to a basketball referee—WHET HIS WHISTLE

87. **Jumbles:** BELLE FAMED UPHELD GAINED
Answer: Why the farmer yelled at the sow—SHE WAS PIGHEADED

88. **Jumbles:** DERBY AFTER ARCADE BAMBOO
Answer: What the company chairman faced at the meeting—A BORED BOARD

89. **Jumbles:** GUILE USURP BUSILY STANZA
Answer: Easy to raise after the garden is readied—BLISTERS

90. **Jumbles:** JUMPY ERASE CROUCH FALLEN
Answer: What the barber experienced while he worked—"SHEAR" JOY

91. **Jumbles:** BOOTH PIPER TYCOON SMUDGE
Answer: Why the fastball hurler sang in the shower—HE HAD A GOOD PITCH

92. **Jumbles:** DAISY BUMPY ANEMIA OVERDO
Answer: What Mom got on her birthday—A BED "SPREAD"

93. **Jumbles:** GUIDE IDIOM FORAGE ACTUAL
Answer: When he saw Grandpa's watch he thought it was—AN OLD "TIMER"

94. **Jumbles:** JUMBO COWER REVERE HORROR
Answer: What the beginner ended up knitting—HER BROW

95. **Jumbles:** COMET VOUCH STOOGE UNPAID
Answer: How the balding politician fared against the young candidate—HE CAME OUT ON "TOP"

185

96. **Jumbles:** FOIST TAKEN DENTAL CANNED
Answer: Always involved in an internet transaction—THE "DOTTED" LINE

97. **Jumbles:** RAJAH GRAVE TEACUP RITUAL
Answer: What the doctor found at the meat counter—THE RIGHT "CURE"

98. **Jumbles:** ELATE MAKER ANYONE PUDDLE
Answer: What the ex–cover girl did when she resumed her career—RE-MODELED

99. **Jumbles:** ANNUL PHONY FRENZY BOTANY
Answer: When the busy pilot ate—ON THE FLY

100. **Jumbles:** DAUNT FLUKE OUTWIT NOVICE
Answer: What the careful ski boat operator did—TOWED THE LINE

101. **Jumbles:** FEIGN LIBEL HELMET TRIPLE
Answer: Another name for evening hours—"LIGHT" TIME

102. **Jumbles:** HANDY NATAL VELVET PIGPEN
Answer: What the smooth-talking conductor ran into—THE END OF THE "LINE"

103. **Jumbles:** ABOVE CROWN FORGET FABLED
Answer: When he rolled a perfect game his opponent was—"BOWLED" OVER

104. **Jumbles:** MOUSY TWEAK CATNIP LEDGER
Answer: An unsolicited call from a broker can result in this—A "STOCK" REPLY

105. **Jumbles:** QUILT FLOUT ZODIAC BEHOLD
Answer: When the icicle fell on his head he was—OUT "COLD"

106. **Jumbles:** STUNG FRANC INTAKE NOZZLE
Answer: What the boss' son used to get his way—"KINFLUENCE"

107. **Jumbles:** FINIS OZONE ANKLET FARINA
Answer: This will cause tires to go up—INFLATION

108. **Jumbles:** GRAIN FLUTE SECEDE JAGUAR
Answer: What the poker players considered his bet—A "GRAND" GESTURE

109. **Jumbles:** PLUSH CASTE HIATUS QUAINT
Answer: The visiting clowns turned the children's ward into this—A "HA-SPITAL"

110. **Jumbles:** ABATE NOISE OBTUSE FERVID
Answer: Found in a buffet-style restaurant—"SEE" FOOD

111. **Jumbles:** COLIC WAGER BANTER AMOEBA
Answer: The angry dancers turned the dance hall into this—A BRAWL ROOM

112. **Jumbles:** KNACK CLUCK TANDEM LEGACY
Answer: What it felt like when she played her melody—A MALADY

113. **Jumbles:** BERET DRONE VERBAL SUBURB
Answer: Another name for a demolition expert—A RUBBLE ROUSER

114. **Jumbles:** JADED FLOOD DECENT OUTLAW
Answer: What he did at the computer store—"DOWN LOADED"

115. **Jumbles:** WHISK TRACT POPLIN ASYLUM
Answer: The old-time clock-maker was known as this—MAN OF THE "HOUR"

116. **Jumbles:** BOOTY HAREM ABUSED CROTCH
Answer: Where the executives met to listen to poetry—IN THE BARD ROOM

117. **Jumbles:** SWAMP SCOUT SUBDUE SOCKET
Answer: You might say he did this when he strolled by the moose—PASSED THE BUCK

118. **Jumbles:** CRANK EPOCH JOVIAL DRUDGE
Answer: What she considered his attempt at conversation—AN "I" OPENER

119. **Jumbles:** VIXEN CHAOS LETHAL DURESS
Answer: Why he never became a good diver—IT WAS OVER HIS HEAD

120. **Jumbles:** JEWEL SHYLY TROPHY OPIATE
Answer: What the young witch learned at school—HOW TO "SPELL"

121. **Jumbles:** GROUP INKED VIOLIN FIXING
Answer: Where the company downsizing put the manager—ON THE "FIRING" LINE

122. **Jumbles:** CYCLE QUOTA TRAGIC IMPACT
Answer: What the inspector considered her working hours—"QUALITY" TIME

123. **Jumbles:** GAUGE MIDGE GIMLET HAZING
Answer: Why did the hungry diner complain about the long wait?—IT WAS EATING HIM

124. **Jumbles:** BALKY LEECH UNSEAT DAMPEN
Answer: What an instructor does at baking school—HELPS THE KNEADY

125. **Jumbles:** GNOME SHINY EMBRYO PICNIC
Answer: The tightwad investor watched this on-line—HIS MONEY

126. **Jumbles:** CHAFF GLAND UNCOIL RAGLAN
Answer: What the comedian was known as for his telephone routine—A CALLING "CARD"

127. **Jumbles:** FELON CAKED DITHER EXCISE
Answer: What he considered the tiny profits from his egg farm—CHICKEN FEED

128. **Jumbles:** DOGMA RURAL ABACUS CHORUS
Answer: What the expert on highways was considered by his peers—A "ROADS" SCHOLAR

129. **Jumbles:** EXERT CANAL FEDORA HANGER
Answer: This happened to the runner who fell in love—HIS HEART RACED

130. **Jumbles:** CHICK CHANT GAMBLE OBLONG
Answer: What the retired barber ended up doing—BEACH COMBING

131. **Jumbles:** HEFTY FAINT ORCHID NEGATE
Answer: Important to get when working in an art gallery—THE HANG OF IT

132. **Jumbles:** DOUSE FATAL SEXTON RADISH
Answer: What Mom ended up with when too much vinegar was poured—"TOSSED" SALAD

133. **Jumbles:** JOUST EIGHT FOSSIL THROAT
Answer: The ambitious photographer decided to—SHOOT FOR THE STARS

134. **Jumbles:** EXILE TEASE DIGEST INVENT
Answer: Investing in property involves this—SITE SEEING

135. **Jumbles:** ALBUM PRONE EXCITE STUPID
Answer: What the sailors did on shore leave—CRUISED

136. **Jumbles:** TONIC BRIAR INSIST EFFIGY
Answer: Where the violin-playing football player ended up—THE FIRST STRING

137. **Jumbles:** THICK MOTIF GOATEE ORATOR
Answer: What junior faced when he flunked the fractions test—THE "AFTER-MATH"

138. **Jumbles:** BILGE LINEN BUZZER WHEEZE
Answer: Why the manager wasn't surprised when the waitresses argued—IT WAS BREWING

139. **Jumbles:** PEONY FLORA PYTHON EVOLVE
Answer: When a relationship sours they're easy to see—OTHER PEOPLE

140. **Jumbles:** WEDGE LEGAL FLABBY VALUED
Answer: What the brothers called their newborn sister—THE BELLE OF THE "BAWL"

141. **Jumbles:** AGATE CHOKE FAUCET ANGINA
Answer: What the artist's portrayal of the show dog was considered—FETCHING

142. **Jumbles:** NOOSE LADLE ZITHER QUAVER
Answer: Getting the most cards on Valentine's Day made her this—THE QUEEN OF HEARTS

143. **Jumbles:** FLUID CRESS SHREWD FROZEN
    Answer: What the overweight empty nesters did—
    DOWNSIZED

144. **Jumbles:** ENEMY DALLY HOMING ESTATE
    Answer: The jeweler's transaction turned out to be
    this—A GEM OF A SALE

145. **Jumbles:** CROUP GULCH FORGER MEMORY
    Answer: Important to keep when the boss gets hot—
    YOUR COOL

146. **Jumbles:** TWEET ADAPT THRIVE UPTOWN
    Answer: What it takes to succeed with a horoscope
    website—A "NET" PROPHET

147. **Jumbles:** DUNCE BLOOD TALLOW DRIVEL
    Answer: Midnight snacks while studying helped him
    become this—WELL "ROUNDED"

148. **Jumbles:** NEEDY CREEL GUTTER CALLOW
    Answer: What the director captured in the movie about
    Hollywood—THE REEL WORLD

149. **Jumbles:** DIRTY FOLIO LOUNGE PILFER
    Answer: What the lioness became when the cubs were
    born—"PRIDE-FULL"

150. **Jumbles:** HURRY PECAN INJURE ATTACH
    Answer: Some spurn this English ritual because it's
    not—THEIR CUP OF TEA

151. **Jumbles:** QUEEN RABBI CLOTHE STICKY
    Answer: What the farm hands turned into after hoeing
    all the fields—"ACHE-ERS"

152. **Jumbles:** ALIVE BURST SUCKLE ENCAMP
    Answer: What the orthodontist saw when he examined
    the patient—PLACES FOR BRACES

153. **Jumbles:** PARTY PRUNE SUNDAE TRYING
    Answer: A plumber's specialty—DRAIN SURGERY

154. **Jumbles:** LOGIC BEIGE JURIST GOBLET
    Answer: What the senator ended up with when his
    daughter got married—THE BILL OF RITES

155. **Jumbles:** BAKED BLOOM NOGGIN NETHER
    Answer: This happened on his first fishing trip—
    HE GOT HOOKED

156. **Jumbles:** BASIS PRIZE JOSTLE BROKEN
    Answer: What he said after he installed the fan—
    "IT'S A BREEZE"

157. **Jumbles:** TWICE LOFTY OUTLET ENOUGH
    Answer: Arctic sailors often do this—
    GO WITH THE FLOE

158. **Jumbles:** DECAY BIPED ENGINE BETRAY
    Answer: What her vegetable patch turned into—
    A GARDEN OF EATIN'

159. **Jumbles:** TYING AUGUR BISECT FESTAL
    Answer: Mom sprayed the new puppies to avoid this—
    "LITTER" BUGS

160. **Jumbles:** GOURD DEMON YEARLY HITHER
    Answer: What the cows did when she rang the dinner
    bell—THE HERD HEARD

161. **Jumbles:** CLOVEN DISCUS MURMUR DENOTE
    FACTOR SOLACE
    Answer: What the hotel manager had when the rowdy
    group arrived—RESERVATIONS

162. **Jumbles:** INFUSE GAIETY HOPPER STYMIE
    INLAID AFRAID
    Answer: What the barber's will ended up doing—
    SPLITTING HEIRS

163. **Jumbles:** UPROAR ARTERY UNFAIR NUANCE
    JACKAL VELLUM
    Answer: Many do this in the fall—TURN OVER AN
    OLD LEAF

164. **Jumbles:** DOMINO ANYWAY HARROW YELLOW
    TIMELY PANTRY
    Answer: What he faced after a sleepless night—
    THE YAWN OF A NEW DAY

165. **Jumbles:** INCOME REBUKE PLACID JUMPER
    TYRANT GLOBAL
    Answer: Where the clown ended up when he let his
    hair grow—UNDER THE BIG "TOP"

166. **Jumbles:** BOYISH LAWYER JINGLE HAUNCH
    UPWARD AVOWAL
    Answer: What the Christmas display turned the kid
    into—A WINDOW "WISHER"

167. **Jumbles:** LUNACY EMERGE FLATLY BARREN
    DABBLE EMBODY
    Answer: Important for a high-wire performer—
    A "BALANCED" MEAL

168. **Jumbles:** HUMBLE RABBIT DEBATE IMPEDE
    INBORN NICETY
    Answer: The villagers said the new clock tower was—
    A TIMELY ADDITION

169. **Jumbles:** GIGGLE KOSHER GRAVEN EGOISM
    NOBODY DROPSY
    Answer: Easily made by a top-notch mimic—
    A GOOD IMPRESSION

170. **Jumbles:** FALLOW HAZARD SUBWAY MAMMAL
    RACIAL OCELOT
    Answer: Paying for a fancy meal can become this—
    HARD TO SWALLOW

171. **Jumbles:** THORAX MODISH AMAZON BEMOAN
    ADAGIO BEAUTY
    Answer: What the couple enjoyed after the wedding—
    THE BONDS OF MATRIMONY

172. **Jumbles:** ALPACA VARIED RATHER THRUSH
    BANISH REFUGE
    Answer: Cutting her tresses gave her this—
    "SHEAR" PLEASURE

173. **Jumbles:** DEVOUR NEPHEW MASCOT GUIDED
    INJURY FUTURE
    Answer: The electrician's favorite subject in night
    school—"CURRENT" EVENTS

174. **Jumbles:** DECADE MOTHER FRIGID ADDUCE
    SPLEEN TREATY
    Answer: This always saddens hunters—
    THE DEER DEPARTED

175. **Jumbles:** DAMAGE GARBLE INVADE PIRACY
    BEDBUG KENNEL
    Answer: A job at a nursery can lead to this—
    A "BUDDING" CAREER

176. **Jumbles:** JARGON ACHING CANYON HOOKUP
    APIECE BROOCH
    Answer: The clerks were reluctant to do this when the
    judge napped in the park—APPROACH THE BENCH

177. **Jumbles:** LANCER MYOPIC TINKLE AMPERE
    JOYFUL MORTAR
    Answer: The salesman sold insurance because it was
    a—COMPANY "POLICY"

178. **Jumbles:** COMEDY FONDLY UNLESS FAMILY
    ENGULF DISARM
    Answer: What junior did when he was caught not doing
    his homework—LEARNED HIS LESSON

179. **Jumbles:** SCHOOL QUENCH FASTEN KNOTTY
    LAVISH IMMUNE
    Answer: Why the sergeant helped the recruit polish his
    boots—HE TOOK A SHINE TO HIM

180. **Jumbles:** BANDIT LACKEY BOILED HANSOM
    NUDISM FACING
    Answer: What the bridge players wanted on the
    cruise—GOOD "DECK" HANDS

Need More Jumbles®?

Order any of these books through your bookseller or call Triumph Books toll-free at 800-335-5323.